Jean Taylor

Macdonald Guidelines

Managing editor
Chester Fisher
Series editor
Jim Miles
Editor
Susan Moore
Designer
Jill Leman
Picture research
Brigitte Arora
Production
Penny Kitchenham

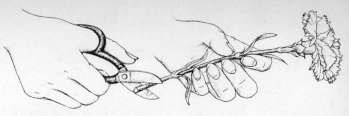

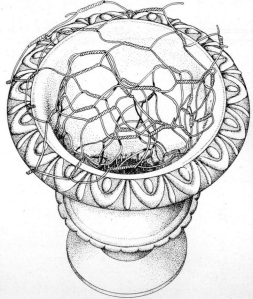

2

Contents

© Macdonald Educational Ltd 1978

First published 1978
Macdonald Educational Ltd
Holywell House, Worship Street,
London EC2A 2EN

ISBN 0 356 06025 X

What is flower arranging?

Why pick flowers to place in containers? It's easy to see that more people can enjoy the beauty of flowers when they are cut and placed in a vase; but why *arrange* flowers? Although flowers can simply be dropped into water without any adjustments, each one can be seen to its best advantage if it is positioned carefully.

Flower arranging needs no inborn talent. It can be learned from a book, or in classes; and a quite acceptable arrangement can be made early on in the process of learning. Our aesthetic awareness can also be height-ened by a knowledge of flower arranging; and as a result the work of artists in other media becomes more easily understood.

Florists and flower arrangers

Florists sell fresh, cut flowers and foliage, and rooted plants, grown at home and abroad in nurseries, gardens and glass-houses. They also stock dried plant material and all kinds of equipment including containers for flower arrangements, and make flowers into bouquets, posies, corsages (or buttonholes, the masculine equivalent), wreaths and sprays. Sometimes they make flower arrangements for customers, for use in a home or for a public room.

Flower arrangers, on the other hand, are not normally concerned with selling flowers. Their main concern is the artistic presentation of flowers and other plant material, either in the home or in public buildings, for regular use or for special occasions. Many people arrange flowers for sheer enjoyment; but others are reimbursed for their work. This includes demonstrating flower arranging, teaching students, judging competitive work, arranging flowers

◀ One of the oldest uses of flowers as an art form is for religious purposes. Large arrangements, like this twenty-foot column arranged by the York Flower Club in York Minster, are now done, in churches and cathedrals, for flower festivals.

▶ Flowers arranged by the author in the manner of a seventeenth-century European flower painting (see p. 16). Their stems are supported by the narrow neck of the simple container.

for occasions such as weddings and social events, and freelance work in hotels and restaurants.

Occasions and places

Flowers have been carried and arranged for special ceremonies and events from earliest times. Nowadays they are seen at all kinds of occasion, from state functions to church services and private dinners. Bouquets are presented and carried, and corsages and buttonholes are worn, at many events. Privately, flowers are given as expressions of love, sympathy or gratitude; or simply as a thoughtful gesture.

There are many rooms in addition to those in private homes where flowers can be arranged to make our surroundings more attractive.

Hospitals are always full of flowers sent by well-wishers to patients. The flowers are arranged by nurses, by patients or by voluntary workers or are delivered already arranged by a florist or friend.

◀ In public places and homes alike, flowers should be arranged to suit their surroundings. This pedestal arrangement is designed to match both the proportions and the atmosphere of the entrance foyer in a big hotel. Large-scale plant material is used and the tall marble pedestal itself reflects the size of the marble pillars.

Churches traditionally have flower arrangements for the Sunday services and in some churches they are left in place throughout the week. The flowers are normally arranged by members of a church flower guild who use flowers donated by other members of the church or provided from local gardens.

Shops and offices that display flowers and plants can have them maintained by contract with a florist; but in smaller establishments an interest is often taken by a staff member.

Hotels and restaurants sometimes employ one person to arrange the flowers or the job may be contracted with a florist. Occasionally it is an additional responsibility of a member of staff.

Civic halls and offices use flower arrangements on special occasions and these are the responsibility of the local parks and gardens department.

▲ Most churches are decorated with flower arrangements at least once a week.

▼ This simple arrangement is styled to suit a small room in a private home.

Styles and shapes

Many flowers can be used in a design or few or, surprisingly, no flowers at all because sometimes such things as seed-heads or leaves are used. Flowers can be massed to give an effect of colour and texture or they can be arranged with more restraint to emphasize shape and movement. Personal tastes vary and so does architecture and interior decoration. Different styles in flower arrangement suit different styles of interiors. Shapes also vary; and a position such as a low table will need a different shape from a high ledge.

► Strelitzias, driftwood and aspidistra leaves arranged by the author in modern style in a stoneware container.

Arrangements can match very varied styles of surroundings. A sparse modern design may suit a modern interior, and so too may an abstract arrangement—that is, one that does not use plant material naturalistically—while in the kitchen a simple arrangement in a jug might look best. The position of the flowers is also important: on a low table they should be arranged to be appreciated from above; in a narrow alcove a tall slender design is best; and heavy-looking furniture can be complemented by a mass of flowers.

◄ An arrangement for a wedding reception by Julia Clements.

► An abstract design by Barbara Rogers, using painted ivy stems, dried flowers of achillea, magnolia leaves and burnt gorse stems. The background was painted to harmonize with the design; and pottery discs support the plant material.

Material for arrangement

The materials of an art or craft are called 'the medium'. The medium of flower arranging is collectively called 'plant material' and this term covers any part of a plant, fresh or dried.

Finding plant material

There are sources for plant material everywhere, both in city and country. People with gardens can grow plenty of material, including plants that are especially suitable for cutting because they last well in water or are an interesting shape or colour. Lists of plants for adding to the garden can be found on pp.80–81.

Those living in the country can find material easily because the hedgerows, fields, ditches, lakesides and shores provide a wealth of plants for cutting and collecting.

It is important to remember that many wild plants are now protected by law; but there are numerous varieties that grow in profusion and are not listed as rare. There are also many objects such as cones, grasses, ferns, bulrushes and weathered wood—generally but not entirely accurately, known as driftwood—for collection.

Living in a city, being without a garden, or living in a part of the world where there are extremes of climate, need not prevent anyone from making flower arrangements. A permanent collection of dried and preserved leaves, flowers, seedheads, cones, grasses, bark, branches and driftwood can soon be made. These can form the basis for designs on their own or to which it is easy to add a few flowers if something fresh is wanted. Flowers can be bought from florists in all cities and towns. And market stalls and barrows often sell flowers. Garden centres and nurseries on the boundaries of urban districts are also very useful.

Many travellers collect material when on holiday abroad. Some countries have laws which prevent importing rooted and, in a a few places, fresh cut plant material but dried seedheads and driftwood are normally allowed into any country.

Friends are often good sources of supply and many will share their gleanings or exchange plant material. A seeing eye for flower-arranging materials very quickly develops and most experienced people are great hoarders. It is more usual for them to have too much in a collection than too little to work with.

◀ Fresh flowers and foliage are on sale at shops like this even in smaller towns.

▲ A garden may provide the greatest variety of plant material for cutting for use in arrangements.

Garden plants

New plants can take some time to become established and so it is important to add plants to a garden, especially for cutting for flower arrangements, as soon as possible.

Foliage is of great importance. Flowers can always be bought but foliage is more difficult to find. The basis for many good arrangements is leaves, with the later addition of a few flowers. A pleasing design can also be made using foliage on its own.

Shrubs and trees are a long-term investment for a new garden. Evergreens should be planted but can take a few years to mature. Perennials provide excellent cut foliage in a short time and annual flowers give quick results. Seedsmen offer collections of flowers for cutting and some for drying.

Which plant material?

FLOWERS

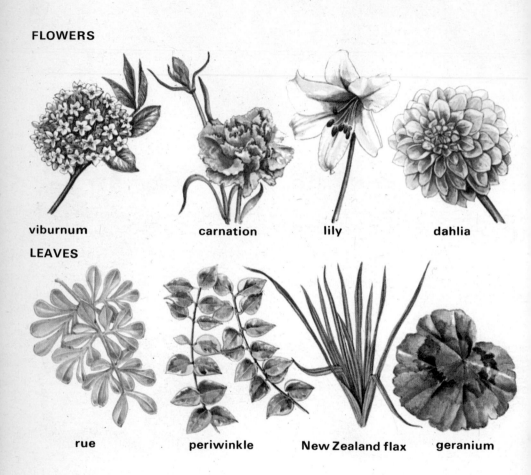

viburnum   carnation   lily   dahlia

LEAVES

rue   periwinkle   New Zealand flax   geranium

All parts of plants are now used in making designs. The name 'flower arrangement' is limited and out of date, but with the exception of 'floral art' which is sometimes used, no other name has been generally adopted.

In addition to flowers, arrangers use branches, bark, pieces of tree trunk, roots, leaves, seedheads, fruits, nuts, cones, bracts, stems, catkins, grasses, vegetables, ferns and weathered wood. They are used alone or in a variety of combinations. They can be fresh and living, dried and preserved. Sometimes fresh and dried and preserved are used in one arrangement.

Arranging is a matter of first selecting and then of assembling the parts of plants

CATKINS AND SEEDHEADS

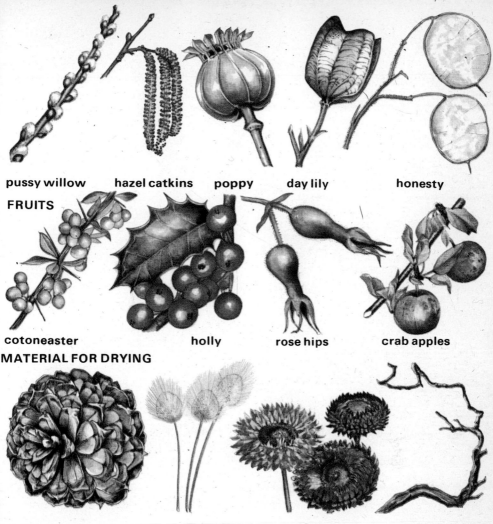

pussy willow   **hazel catkins**   **poppy**   **day lily**   **honesty**

FRUITS

cotoneaster   **holly**   **rose hips**   **crab apples**

MATERIAL FOR DRYING

Scots pine cone   **hare's tail**   **strawflower**   **weathered wood**

that seem to go well together. Size, colour, shape and texture, which are qualities of all objects, are the main considerations.

For example round and elongated shapes together provide a contrast; rough and smooth textures near each other add variety. Sizes look better if they are closely related. Colours can be used that provide dramatic contrast such as yellow and violet or they can be chosen to give a softer, more closely related harmony as in a variety of greens.

Much of the art of flower arranging lies in the initial choice of flowers and leaves and other parts of plants that combine well with each other and with the container in which they are placed.

Flower arranging in history

Because of the tremendous interest now prevailing in flower arranging, it is often considered to be a modern art. But this is not so. Cutting flowers and placing them in receptacles of water is as old as civilization, although flower decoration has taken many forms through the ages. The reason for it has also varied and although its use in early times was mainly religious and symbolic, it also developed as a domestic art in the Middle Ages.

It is now clear that Neanderthal man, 46,000 years ago, was a creature who was responsive to the beauty of flowers. Botanical evidence has proved that an ancient grave found at Shanidar was bedecked with flowers.

It was an early pagan practice to garland sepulchres with flowers and although early Christians did not 'crown the dead' they saw a relationship between flowers and death and felt that flowers were symbolic of the garden of Paradise. This led to the floral decoration of the tombs of saints and later of all Christians.

Each period in history reflects in its arts the prevailing social conditions and artistic trends. Consequently flowers have been used in many styles.

The early Egyptians made vases especially for flowers, in particular the lotus, sacred to the goddess Isis. They arranged them with geometrical precision, and bowls were used at banquets, borne in processions and buried with the dead. A small circlet of spring flowers was found on the forehead of Tutankhamun when his tomb was opened.

In ancient Greece flowers and leaves were fashioned into garlands and head wreaths which were exchanged or given on many occasions. Professional garland-makers were members of many households. There is, however, little evidence that flowers were cut and placed in Greek vases, which were used for food and drink.

The use of rose blossoms and petals was lavish in Roman festivities but after the decline of the Roman Empire flower art disappeared in Europe until the Middle Ages.

◄ In an ancient Egyptian tomb one detail from a painting of 1380 BC represents designs of cut flowers.

▲ A sixteenth-century scroll painting from Japan.

▶ Detail from an eighteenth-century mural in the Topkapi Palace, Istanbul.

Two trends

There have been two main trends in the development of flower arranging, one from Europe and one from the Orient. Flower arranging has been part of the way of life in China and Japan for over a thousand years. Early Chinese designs of restrained simplicity reveal a love and respect for natural beauty which along with Buddhism was passed to Japan. Although originally a temple art and not a home art in Japan until the fifteenth century, the practice of arranging flowers reached a great height in the eighteenth century when rules and symbolism became entwined with the art. *Ikebana* still plays a large part in the life of Japan

◀ *Flowers in a Glass Vase,* by the Dutch painter Jacob van Walscappelle (1644-1727), showing flowers of more than one season.

▶ Victorian styles of arrangement were often dense and elaborate compared with styles used before and since.

and has become international in the last twenty-five years.

The second trend, with a more lavish use of flowers, stems from Europe. In the medieval world the church was the centre of community life with church festivals a major event, preceded by processions when flowers were strewn across roads and traditional greenery was used in abundance in churches. Garlands were hung from roofs, walls and pillars and red roses were used on Corpus Christi Day. The ancient symbolism of flowers continued although the meaning of a flower varied from country to country and age to age. It was an important way of conveying messages to a large number of people who could not read. Renaissance paintings show vases of cut flowers, especially *Lilium candidum*, symbolic of the Madonna, and the rose representing virginity.

The seventeenth-century Flemish and Dutch masters of still life left many exquisite paintings of flower arrangements which are an inspiration to present-day arrangers. The designs were assembled from reference drawings of flowers and were botanical records and exercises in the use of colour. They were not painted from actual arrangements and flowers of all seasons are shown together. However they reflect a great love for flowers, in many colours in an exuberant style quite different from the Oriental.

From books, paintings, furniture, carpets, murals, wood carvings, mosaics and other antiquities it is possible to make a study of the various periods. Over the centuries artists in all mediums have used arrangements of flowers for ornamentation, leaving a record of the style of container, varieties of flowers, and shapes of designs.

Present-day flower arrangers study period styles and make arrangements that give the atmosphere and capture the spirit of a chosen period. When possible they use authentic containers but when these are not available they use present-day materials to simulate the design. An especial favourite is the Victorian style because in that age the interest was very strong. Every respectable young lady was expected to be capable of arranging flowers because, as written in Godey's *Lady's Book* in 1855, 'they employ the hand, delight the eye and inform and edify the mind and unlike many artificial objects the enjoyment and instruction they afford is within the reach of all'.

17

Flower arranging today

For many centuries and in many countries flowers have been cut and placed in containers of water, in dwellings, temples, shrines and public buildings, either for symbolic reasons or for decoration (see pp. 14–15). This work was carried out by individuals, householders, priests, slaves or employees working alone or in small groups.

But the idea of a larger number of flower arrangers meeting to enjoy the activity of arranging flowers together, on the scale practised in many countries today, is a new one.

Clubs

The formation of clubs in small neighbourhoods, villages, towns and cities began in the 1950s and gained impetus particularly in the United States and the United Kingdom.

With today's speedy communications, easy world travel and wide distribution of books, slides and films translated into many languages, knowledge of flower-arranging activities increases and clubs have continued to open all over the world, often started by someone who has seen their success in another country.

Activities

Flower arranging and horticulture are the main interests, but to a varying extent. In some clubs flower arranging is the main subject; others emphasize horticulture and some take an equal interest in both. Membership is usually open, and available to men and women of all ages. Some clubs have junior sections.

Most clubs hold regular meetings at least once a month when demonstrations, lectures and practices are held. There are also social events, group holidays and visits to places and events of special interest, such as

◀ Flower arrangement shows are staged by flower clubs. These arrangements are being prepared for display outside the entrance to a local exhibition.

famous gardens. Many clubs have libraries, and sales tables for equipment, and sell publications.

In clubs where flower arranging is the major interest, members have looked for various ways of practising their skills other than at home or in the club. The result is two major activities:

1 The decoration of buildings, which involves groups working together to decorate stately houses, cathedrals, churches, art galleries, museums and civic buildings, to exercise the members' skill in flower arranging, show the public what can be achieved and raise money for the restoration of old buildings and for charity.

2 Competitions in flower arranging when exhibits are judged, awards are made and the public attend. These are called

▲ Classes in flower arranging are held by flower arrangement clubs and by, educational establishments. They cater for all levels of ability and experience.

flower shows. They often combine competitive and non-competitive work and are sponsored by a club, several clubs working together or a national association. An example is the National Festival of Flower Arrangement held each year in different parts of the United Kingdom, which attracts international exhibitors.

There are also flower arranging sections in many horticultural shows, both large and small. Some of these attract world-wide attention such as the Chelsea Flower Show in London, the Garden Club of Toronto Show and others in Philadelphia and Monaco.

Associations

As the number of clubs in any country increases, associations of clubs are formed, usually nationally. They give assistance to smaller groups, encourage new clubs, promote a wider interest in flower arranging and horticulture, hold major shows and exhibitions and liaise with similar and related organizations elsewhere. Often they arrange the training and testing of judges, lecturers, demonstrators and teachers.

As an example, there are about 400,000 members of approximately 14,000 Garden Clubs, with 64,000 junior members, in the United States. The clubs are often in small neighbourhoods and flower arranging and horticulture, with conservation, are of equal importance to them. They are affiliated through regional and state associations to the National Council of State Garden Clubs. The National Association of Flower Arrangement Societies of Great Britain has about 100,000 members in over 1,200 clubs, with flower arranging the major interest. The Women's Institutes and the Townswomen's Guild are also active in this sphere. Horticulture is a supporting activity. There are also national associations in New Zealand, Australia, Italy, France, Belgium, Ireland and Zimbabwe, and others are forming. Many islands have clubs, such as Bermuda, Malta and Cyprus. There are clubs in Africa, Mexico, South and Central America, Canada, the Caribbean, the Lebanon, the Philippines, West Germany, Austria and the Middle East. As yet there is no world federation but judges, demonstrators, lecturers and teachers travel worldwide and friendship through flowers is now international.

◀ In competitive flower arrangement shows entries interpret a story, atmosphere or scene. Here, Winnie Simpson exhibits 'Cries of London' at a national festival.

Church flowers

Flower arrangements are placed weekly in most churches throughout the world, arranged by church flower guilds or by individual arrangers. Sometimes special festivals are held in cathedrals and in churches of all sizes. Some are organized by a local flower club or clubs and others are the responsibility of church flower arrangers, with local club members taking part. They encourage an important spirit in the community and are very popular with the public. Many of the arrangements are decorative but at the same time arrangers avoid concealing the permanent features of the church. Sometimes flowers are combined with embroidered copes and altar frontals. Other arrangements interpret the Church calendar, the Scriptures, the history of the church or town, ancient and local craftsmen, poets or artists.

Classes

Classes cover all aspects of flower arranging and vary in length and required ability. They are organized by individuals, clubs, national and regional associations and educational authorities. Some lead to examinations and certificates of attainment.

In Japan classes have been conducted for centuries and there are many schools for the study of the ancient art of *Ikebana* or Japanese flower arrangement. Ikebana International has associated chapters and study groups throughout the world.

Western arrangements

The term 'Western' has been adopted to distinguish between *Ikebana* and other styles and practices. It does not refer to the Western part of the world but is a collective term for styles from classical to abstract. Many flower arrangers study both.

Basic skills

It is easy enough to cut flowers in the garden, or buy a bunch from a florist, and to place the stems in a container of water. However by taking a little more care you can make flowers last longer, and their stems can be correctly supported so that each flower appears to its best advantage and the whole arrangement looks more attractive. These abilities and a few other skills are easy to learn and are the basis on which to build the artistic quality of a flower arrangement.

Conditioning

This is the term used by flower arrangers for the preparation of plant material before it is arranged in a container of water to make it last well. There are various methods to learn, according to the type of plant stem.

Some plants are not suitable for cutting and no amount of preparation will prevent them wilting. A few flowers can be difficult and need special care. A knowledge of this soon grows with experience. Having spent time arranging flowers it is so much better to have them last well and to have made the right choice of flowers in the first place.

Mechanics

The foundation of a good flower arrangement is firm 'mechanics'. This is the term for anything that supports the stem in position and prevents a flower from falling over. It refers both to the equipment used and to the methods of using it.

The mechanics for an arrangement vary according to the type of stem, the shape of the container and the style of an arrangement. There are not many alternatives and experience soon helps you to select suitable mechanics quickly and also to conceal them in the completed design.

Grooming and trimming

Plant material is not always clean or in perfect condition and an arrangement looks better when damaged and dirty parts of plants are removed or cleaned. This gives a well-groomed, professional appearance.

Trimming away unwanted parts of a branch or reducing a cluster of crowded flowers is one of the secrets of good design. In Japanese flower arranging, especially, it is greatly emphasized.

◀ After buying a bunch of flowers, first cut the ties and loosen the flowers.

▲ Cut flowers should have their stems trimmed again before being placed in lukewarm water.

Drying

Plant material often dries naturally on the plant out of doors: but weather damage can be avoided if plants are cut at the correct time and dried indoors. It also gives better colour retention. Flowers, seedheads and a very few leaves can be dried by hanging them up in dry air.

Flowers can also be dehydrated by burying them in a desiccant. This absorbs the water from the petals and a slightly shrunken but colourful flower remains.

Pressing

This term refers to drying plant material under a weight or in a flower press. The results are flat but can be used to make flower pictures.

Preserving

This term is normally used for preserving fresh plant material, using glycerine. This is an ideal treatment for many types of foliage. It preserves their shape but changes the colour to a shade of brown. Only a few flowers can be preserved in this way. A stock of preserved and dried plant material is especially useful during cold, wet or very hot seasons when plant material is in short supply or expensive. It is also invaluable to anyone who needs a supply of plant material for arrangements but who has no garden.

Making plaques, pictures and swags

The methods of making these can soon be learnt, resulting in long-lasting work with a professional appearance.

Weathered wood treatment

Roots, chunks of wood of a variety of size and shape, branches, woody stems and cross-cuts can be used with flowers and foliage in arrangements. Wood needs treatment before it is used in the house, and there are particular ways of supporting it.

Wiring

This is a skill necessary for the florist making bouquets, corsages and wreaths which need wiring; but the flower arranger too sometimes has to wire a dried or preserved leaf, a pine cone or a seedhead; a floppy stem can also need wiring.

Transporting flowers

Flowers are normally fragile and need careful handling in order to remain undamaged. There are ways of packing them so that they travel well (see p. 30).

A first try

If you have not tried arranging flowers before, buy a bunch of inexpensive flowers or pick some in the

garden. They should be left out of water for as little time as possible, otherwise they may wilt and become difficult to revive.

Fill a deep bucket with tepid water. Using scissors, cut any ties, and gently loosen the flowers. Then cut off about 2 cm of the stem ends. This removes any

seal that may have formed while the stem has been out of water and which prevents the intake of water. Sometimes it is easier to snip the stem ends off while the bunch is still tied up. Next place the stems in the bucket of water.

Meanwhile find a household jug and fill it with

▲ Spring flowers arranged by the author in a pewter jug with a few leaves inserted first to support their stems.

tepid water almost to the top. Before adding the flowers, put in some leaves with strong stems, picked from the garden or bought, with the flowers, from the

► To make a simple arrangement first place sprays of leaves in the container; then add the flowers, with their stems cut at different lengths and the heads turned in different directions.

florist. These will partially fill the opening of the jug and form a network which helps to support the flower stems. The leaves can stand above the rim of the jug.

Place the flowers in the jug one at a time. Soon, because the opening is filled up, the flowers stand in position. At this stage you can begin to 'arrange' them. If they still seem loose add more leaves or a wedge of tissues to hold them in place.

An arrangement usually looks better when the flowers are turned to face different directions. The centre ones can face forwards, the side ones outwards, and those at the back backwards. In other words you see the backs of the flowers in the rear of the jug. All sides of flowers are interesting to look at, and a shop-window effect is avoided when flowers are turned to look in different directions. Try not to squash flower heads together, because when slightly separated, with space in between, each one can be seen more clearly.

Now pull some of the top centre flowers up by holding the stem and gently pulling upwards. This is a posy

style of arrangement and very informal, but it makes a colourful accent in a room.

A narrow-necked vase

This is one of the ancient shapes used for flowers, because the narrow neck gives natural support Curved stems look more graceful, but this shape of vase can also hold straight stems. Leaves placed in the vase beforehand are unnecessary for support but one or two large, plain leaves like geranium can be added to soften the hard-looking rim of the container. The water soon reduces in the neck of the vase, so be sure to add some now and again.

A shallow bowl

This is useful for the centre of a table used for a seated meal. However the wide cavity needs many flowers to fill it. Sticky tape is the answer if you have no other

equipment. Criss-cross it in a lattice, leaving square spaces big enough to take the stem of a flower. Take about 1 cm of tape over the sides, making sure that the bowl is quite dry on the outside. Place flowers and leaves in each space and add some leaves round the edge to conceal the ends of the tape. The stems must be cut to about the height of the container, otherwise they will not stand up.

A deep bowl

A deep bowl with a wide opening takes a mass of flowers unless the cavity is reduced. This can be done with a jam jar of water placed in the centre to hold the flower stems. It will be concealed by the outer bowl. A ring of plasticine pressed on the base of the jam jar will prevent it from slipping —but remember plasticine only adheres to dry surfaces.

Making an arrangement last

When time and money have been spent on making an arrangement it is important to condition the cut plant material so that it has a long life.

Methods of doing this vary according to a number of things; in particular, the parts and varieties of plants that you intend to use.

The life of flowers varies, from weeks to hours. The florists' trade deals only with long-lasting flowers, and with experience flower arrangers soon learn which garden flowers also last well. Many flowers need no special treatment; others benefit from some initial preparation.

Although nothing can stop the eventual fading of flowers, wilting from lack of water can easily be prevented. Flowers can also last longer with special treatment. The methods used concern:

1 Filling stems with water.

2 Lessening or reducing dehydration.

3 Adding products to the water.

FILLING STEMS

When water is no longer supplied by a parent plant the cut stems must receive it from another source. It is easy to place them in a container of water. However this does not guarantee that they take it up. Some stems need preparation. This is decided by the stem structure. However, all cut stems whether from florist or garden, whatever their structure, should have about 2 cm cut off the end, using either a pair of scissors or a knife. This is because a seal forms over the cut end to 'heal' it as soon as it is exposed to air. This seal can prevent the uptake of water. It can be beneficial to cut the end under water. Cutting also helps to remove any air block that may have been set up by an inrush of air when the stem was first cut.

Nothing further need be done to flowers prepared and sold by a florist, but garden flowers need treatment according to the stem.

Hard stems, as on roses, should be slit for 2 cm, using a knife or scissors. This exposes the inner tissue.

Soft stems, as on daffodils, need no preparation.

Woody stems such as on lilac should be slit. About 4 cm of the outside covering should first be peeled off or scraped away, using a knife.

Leaking stems ooze a white fluid called latex, a solution of rubber. This forms an impermeable layer when dry. Hold the ends in a match or gas jet flame for a minute or so to prevent further flow and to char the rubbery material already exuded.

Hollow stems, as those of lupin and delphinium, can be filled with water, using a small watering can, and then plugged with cotton wool. If a shorter stem is needed it should be cut under water.

All garden flowers, unless with soft stems, benefit from a few hours, preferably overnight, in a bucket of deep, warm water placed in a cool, dim place such as an outhouse or garage. The stems will then fill with water.

LESSENING DEHYDRATION

Water evaporates into the air, and the drier the air the more rapidly this occurs. Just as wet washing dries in a warm, dry atmosphere, flower petals and leaves lose water to the surrounding air. When this happens faster than the stem can take up water, especially when the flower has many petals or the stem has many leaves, the plant wilts.

Wilting can be avoided if a damp atmosphere is provided with an occasional fine spray of water around the flowers (see p. 30). Positions such as in a sunny window, on a radiator, near an open fire or television set, should be avoided. Draughts also dry flowers quickly. They last best in cool rooms, because dehydration, and ageing, are slowed down.

◀ Whatever the plant, a cut stem must always have a short length removed before it is put in water.

▶ Stems that leak, such as those of poppies (right) and euphorbias, should be singed.

◀ Lilac stems and others with a hard exterior must be scraped and slit lengthwise to help intake of water.

Foliage should be submerged for a few hours or overnight to fill it with water and cut down dehydration. This is the normal treatment for all but grey leaves. Tiny hairs give an effect of greyness; when waterlogged, the leaves look green, and drip.

Flowers on stems that carry many leaves, such as mock-orange, soon wilt because there are many transpiring surfaces. All available water goes to the flowers if the leaves are removed.

Picking flowers

It is usually best to pick at the end of the day when flowers contain maximum food reserves made in daylight. Soak in deep water overnight before arranging. In hot weather pick early in

▼ Boiling water can prevent formation of slime, which may block stems. Pour the water into an unbreakable container before putting the flowers in it.

the morning or late in the evening to avoid rapid wilting.

Water temperature

Warm water comfortable to the hands is better than cold, and moves into the stems more easily. Boiling water is useful but only about 2 cm of stem should be placed in it. It moves quickly into the stem and is helpful to flowers that wilt quickly such as garden roses and wild flowers. It also sterilizes, and so reduces micro-organisms that make slime and block the water channels. It kills the cells in the stem end and prevents sugars and other nutrients from channelling out and producing slime. The stem can be left in the hot water until it cools, but flowers should be placed out of steam or protected with paper or a cloth.

Topping up

All arrangements should be topped up to replace the water taken up by the flowers and transpired to the air. The smaller the receptacle of water, the larger the number of flowers and the drier the room, the more often topping up must take place.

Wilted plant material

If plant material flops before its life is over, it can often be revived. Remove from the arrangement and submerge leaves in deep warm water for two hours. Flowers can be floated in a bowl or sink of warm water (see p. 30). Snipping off 2 cm of stem can remove any air block. Placing the stem end in boiling water then starts water moving quickly into the flower again. Finally, place in deep warm water in a dim, cool room.

ADDITIVES

Water need not be changed if mild disinfectant is added. This is unnecessary with short-lived flowers but prevents unpleasant water with long-lived chrysanthemums. There are also commercial additives to help flowers last, with four solutions for different plant material.

No simple rules apply to other additives. What works for one person does not work for another, because tap water differs in composition or flowers are not picked in the same variety or at the same age. It is best to try each idea for yourself and to keep records.

AGE OF FLOWERS AND LEAVES

Always buy or pick flowers that are not fully mature to give a longer vase life. (See pp. 82–7 for long-lived flowers and good buys at the florist.) Young leaves, however, do not last well

and soon wilt despite initial submerging.

Forcing flowers

Flowering branches with large buds can be cut and placed in hot water in a warm place to open the flowers quickly. This is successful with spring flowers including forsythia, almond, apple, cherry, plum, pear, jasmine, lilac and magnolia.

Retarding flowers

The development of flowers can be retarded for up to a week in a refrigerator. Place the soaked stems and the flowers in a polythene bag and tie it up. Short-stemmed flowers such as orchids can

be placed in boxes with lids. For up to a day flowers can be left uncovered in a jug of water in the refrigerator.

SPECIAL TREATMENT

Some flowers need other preparation.

Long spikes of flowers curve if left lying horizontally for more than an hour or two. Unless curves are wanted, they are better placed upright.

Berries shrivel in a dry room; but protection can be given by spraying with clear varnish or hair lacquer.

Alliums belong to the onion family and hot water increases their smell. It has the same effect on kale.

▼ Flowers with hollow stems can be prevented from wilting by having their stems filled with water, using a funnel.

▼ To prevent bulrushes releasing their clouds of seeds, spray them with hair lacquer or any colourless varnish.

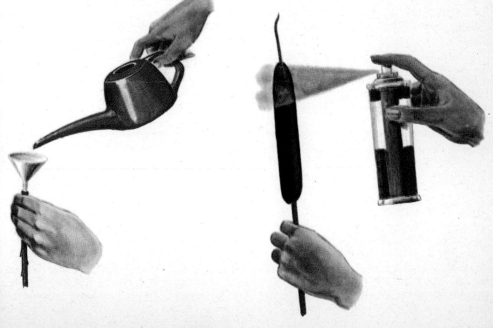

Bougainvilleas, hydrangeas, violets and clematis should be submerged for a few hours.

Bulrushes (reed-mace), grasses and fluffy seedheads should be sprayed with hair lacquer or clear varnish to prevent 'blowing'.

Hyacinth, tulips and zinnias often have heavy flowers which are better supported with a florist's stub wire pushed up the centre of the stem as far as the flower.

Lilies have anthers which stain clothing; these should be cut off, using scissors.

Gerberas should always have the boiling water treatment as they easily wilt.

Hellebores only last when cut in the fruit stage.

Laburnum, lilac, mockorange, bougainvillea, bells of Ireland and wild flowers should be defoliated.

Mimosa should be kept in a polythene bag in a cool place until arranged.

Hippeastrums (usually called amaryllis) need the support of a long stick placed in their hollow stems.

Water lilies can be held open if melted wax is dropped around the centre of the flowers.

Strelitzias (bird-of-paradise) have a number of flowers that can be gently eased out of their sheaths.

Gardenia petals mark if handled with dry fingers.

Pine cones can be wired for placing in an arrangement if first opened by drying. Then place two stub wires, on either side and parallel, into the lower scales. Twist to-

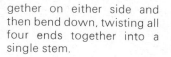

gether on either side and then bend down, twisting all four ends together into a single stem.

Transporting plant material

Pack previously soaked leaves in a polythene bag tied at the end. Flowers should be packed in a cardboard box without polythene. They can support each other or be held up by rolls of paper. For short journeys they can be transported in a bucket of water.

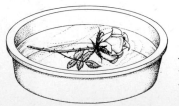

▲ An arrangement can be sprayed with water to prevent wilting.

Grooming

Florists' flowers are normally in perfect condition; but garden plant material can be dirty. Swish foliage in warm water containing detergent. Stubborn dirt can be wiped off with a cloth. Dirty flowers can be washed gently. If necessary remove them, together with any damaged parts.

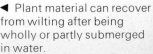

◀ Plant material can recover from wilting after being wholly or partly submerged in water.

Trimming plant material

Before being used in an arrangement plant material may be trimmed to remove damaged leaves, branches or flowers. Trimming may also improve the appearance of its shape. This is one of the important skills of Japanese flower arrangement, and students are taught from the first to trim away parts of the plant to achieve a beautiful design.

Branches being trimmed for a flower arrangement should be simplified so that one main branch remains and all the others are subsidiary. Many smaller branches can be removed entirely, to achieve a more streamlined look. Flowers are often crowded on a stem so that each shape cannot be seen clearly. Some flowers should be removed to give the others clear space around each one. The flowers cut off can be used lower in the design. Spray chrysanthemums, especially, need trimming.

Leaves often crowd each other and give a muddled appearance to the design. Remove overlapping leaves so that each shape is clear. It is well worth practising the trimming of plant material for good design.

Trimming plant material can also be one aspect of grooming. Damaged flowers and leaves should be cut off or trimmed, using flower scissors. An arrangement of damaged plant material looks very untidy. Leaves that grow low down on a stem and that will be under water when arranged in a container should also be cut off. If left they soon decay under water and slime results, reducing the life of the flowers.

▼ Cut away any damaged or crowded leaves.

▲ Trim branches to emphasize the main line.

▲ Remove crowded flowers to show heads separately.

Containers

A container made to hold flowers was formerly called a vase. Nowadays all kinds of receptacles are used for stem ends whether intended for flowers or not. They do not have to be waterproof because they can be lined with polythene or a second container. Expensive and elaborate vases are unnecessary, since flowers can look equally beautiful in simple shapes of a suitable colour. An infinite variety of containers can be found in households, shops and markets; and they can also be made or contrived at home.

Shape

It is useful to make a collection of different shapes of container, so that you have scope for a variety of styles. Tall containers with a stem show off the lower flowers and leaves, which can be arranged to flow downwards gracefully. Low bowls or other shallow containers are useful for table arrangements. Modern stoneware with simple shapes suits present-day interiors, and classical shapes go well in traditional and period homes.

Colour

This is important, largely because brightly coloured containers tend to dominate the flowers. Muted colours, including the browns, dull greens, greys, soft blues and beiges, show off the brighter colours of the flowers and are more versatile. White is lovely with white flowers but with other colours it can seem detached from the arrangement. Black can be effective with darker flowers and dramatic with a white arrangement. Colours of the earth are good because they repeat the effect given when flowers are growing outside.

Texture

The texture of containers should be considered, because shiny surfaces can detract from the appearance of the flowers. Matt surfaces, either rough or smooth, are usually better.

Unseen containers

Food and baking tins, painted with emulsion or with black or green blackboard paint, are invaluable for this use. They should be deep enough to hold plenty of water and the supports for stems. Plant material, or other containers such as a box or basket, can be used to conceal them.

Candlecups

Candlesticks, bottles, oil and electric lamp bases, narrow-necked vases and metal figurines can all be converted into containers by using candle-cups. They are available in different sizes and can be attached permanently with an adhesive or temporarily with plasticine.

Home-made containers

These can be made of pottery; or meat tins and bottles can be given a variety of surfaces with paint and sand, string, Fablon or fabrics.

Bases

A collection of bases is most useful. A base is anything on which a container stands. It has the functional use of preventing damage to the surface it is placed on, and it can also be a part of the design.

Any size, shape, colour or texture of base can be used, to suit the flower arrangement. The great advantage of a base is that it protects furniture from scratches and water marks. In addition it can add to the design by giving visual weight at the bottom. Combined with a painted food tin to hold the flower stems it can provide an economical but attractive setting for flowers.

Muted colours are better than bright ones, which compete with the flower colours. A base, in the same way as a container, should be used as a background for the flowers. A collection can soon be made to include straw, rush and bamboo mats, brass and wooden trays and plates, cross-cuts of polished or natural wood, pieces of marble, trivets, wooden stands, and slate and stone from the countryside. Cakeboards can be given a slip-cover of fabric, so that a variety of colours and textures of this kind can be collected.

Rough surfaces that can scratch furniture should have felt glued on to the bottom. It is important that whatever is used as a base should be level, otherwise the container will not stand safely. Also the style should be suitable for the style of the arrangement. With a naturalistic design, for example, a slate base might be appropriate.

Equipment

Equipment for flower arrangement is not expensive; and whereas cheap and attractive bases and containers can readily be improvised, some implements or equipment may be useful or necessary to buy from the start.

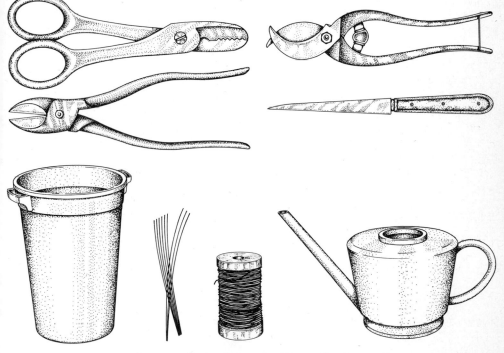

For soaking stems before arranging the flowers, a bucket is necessary. One with a handle on either side is better than one with a single handle, since flowers may be damaged if kept in this type.

Flower scissors are better for cutting flowers than household scissors. They have short, blunt blades with one serrated edge to make it easier to cut stems. There is also a nick at the base for snipping light wire. They will need oiling sometimes. Wire-cutters are useful but not essential. Secateurs are necessary for cutting thick, woody stems; and for scraping woody stems you will want a small knife from the kitchen.

Supports for flower stems are usually needed and are described in detail, with their uses, on pp. 36-44. A reel of wire is essential for securing some supports; and for heavy flowers stub wire is sometimes needed. Plasticine or a similar compound made specially for flower arranging is necessary for holding supports firmly in position.

A watering can with a slim spout is useful for topping up arrangements.

All this equipment can be obtained easily from florists, garden centres, some department stores and flower club sales tables.

The mechanics

Supports for stems are called by flower arrangers 'the mechanics'. These supports are not usually seen in an arrangement, although in some styles of *Ikebana* they are visible and acceptable.

Holding stems firmly in position in a container is the basis for all flower arranging. Through the centuries various devices have been used. The ancient Chinese cut forked twigs to use as supports for flowers, and the Japanese have become extremely skilled with these. They are fitted into a container in a number of positions. In the early nineteenth century Chinese arrangers devised a copper disc on which a number of nails were glued upside down. The disc was then glued into the container. Flowers were tied into groups and impaled on the nails, and sand was then poured over to conceal the nails. This was the forerunner of what we now call a pinholder or a needlepoint holder, which is often used these days.

The early Egyptians made vases with extra spout-like openings on the sides for stems. Similar containers have been made through the ages in many countries.

Moss, sand and the woody stems of plants have been used to fill vases, and raffia straw and, later, string and wire, for binding stems.

The late Victorians invented a glass 'rose' with many holes in which stems were placed. A few of these can be found now in antique shops. The modern version of this is a block of plastic foam which absorbs and retains water without spillage.

This discovery has made flower arranging easier than ever before, and unusual effects can be achieved which would surprise our ancestors.

Buying foam

Plastic foam is sold under several trade names. 'Oasis' was the first, and apt, title and has been adopted by flower arrangers as the name for all plastic foam whatever the brand. It is made in blocks of several sizes and usually coloured green. Large blocks, wet or dry, can easily be cut to fit a container, using a knife. The cost of a small round to hold a few flowers is less than a cup of coffee in most countries, but more expensive where it must be imported over a long distance.

Oasis can sometimes be used more than once. It is obtainable from florists, garden centres and flower clubs. Care should be taken to buy the type that absorbs water, as others are made to hold only dried stems. Some of these types are coloured brown and others green.

Soaking Oasis

Oasis is very light to carry and store and only becomes

◀ Some plastic foam, for use with cut flowers, absorbs water. It should be stored, if damp, in a polythene bag. Other, usually brown, types are used to support dried plant material. Glass roses were used before plastic foam was invented.

▲ A simple arrangement by Violet Stevenson of annual flowers that can be supported in Oasis.

heavy when full of water. A block weighing 45 g when dry weighs 2 kg after soaking and holds about $1\frac{1}{2}$ litres of water.

With the exception of large arrangements half or one third of a big block is used for the average arrangement placed in a home.

Use a small round or cut a piece from a larger block to suit the size of the chosen container. Small slices are not advisable because they give no stem support and hold little water.

Place the foam in water deeper than itself. As it absorbs water it will slowly sink down. When it is level with the surface of the water it is full. This takes about ten minutes for a block measuring about 23 cm by 11 cm. There are instant foams

available in some countries and these should be soaked according to the manufacturer's instructions. Long soaking is unnecessary for foam and no more water can be taken up once it is full.

Supporting foam

A container with tall sides will support blocks of foam in position. Cut a block that stands about 2 to 4 cm above the container's rim so that stems can be placed in it to flow downwards.

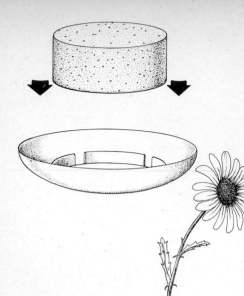

◀ Containers with a built-in rim are designed to hold a standard block of Oasis. When using Oasis it is sometimes best first to establish the height of an arrangement. Stems can be inserted at any angle, especially when the foam stands above the rim of the container.

In a shallow container a foam pinholder can be used. This has about eight long pins placed wide apart and the foam block is held firmly by them (see p. 40 for securing the pinholder).

Some plastic and pottery containers are made now with built-in rims to hold a standard circle of foam. They are inexpensive and sold almost everywhere that foam can be bought. There is also a small plastic four-pronged anchor which is so inexpensive that it can be thrown away with the foam. This is useful for arrangements sent to patients in hospitals.

Stem ends

Stems can easily be pushed into wet Oasis in any position and at any angle. The exceptions are a few very soft stems which bend as they are inserted. Examples are immature leaves and the stems of some mature daffodils. All hard and woody stems go into the foam very easily, but broad branches can make a large hole and then the foam gives way. As the stem goes into Oasis it makes a hole which does not close up if the stem is withdrawn. It is therefore better to leave a stem in the Oasis rather than to keep taking it in and out. Oasis must be discarded when there are many holes and it looks like a sponge. It gives little or no support for stems at this stage and holds little water. After one use it is usually possible to turn it over for a second arrangement.

The more flowers used in an arrangement the bigger should be the block of foam, otherwise the stems soon absorb all the water and the Oasis becomes dry.

After-care

In between use it is better to store the wet foam in a polythene bag to keep it damp.

Once dried out it can be difficult to re-wet, although this can be done sometimes by soaking in water containing detergent or by dropping the block into boiling water for a few minutes.

In a warm, dry room the surface of Oasis soon dries out and so a daily dribble of water applied by means of a thin-spouted watering can is necessary. For this reason it is better when the foam does not fit the container exactly, so that excess water slips into the container and not on the furniture.

Oasis parcels

Oasis can be parcelled in thin polythene to use in a container that does not hold water, such as a wooden box. It can also be used suspended, for a hanging decoration without a container. Tie it up with thin string or reel wire. Strong stems can be pushed through the polythene. A hole can be made first, using a skewer or bradawl, for softer stems to be inserted. If stems are placed on the underside where water collects, however, the water will drip out of the parcel.

Pinholders

A pinholder is a useful and permanent support for stems. It is sometimes called a needlepoint holder, a frog or, in Japan, a *kenzan*. The matter of placing stems on a pinholder is one of the fundamentals of flower arranging and it should be practised, but it is not difficult. It is the most suitable support for sparse arrangements, woody stems and arrangements in shallow containers. In some countries, especially hot ones, pinholders are preferred to Oasis because it is considered that flowers last longer in water than in plastic foam.

Good buys

The more expensive pinholders are usually also the best in the long run. They last indefinitely and do not need replacement. The base should be heavy, and is normally made of lead. The pins should be long and embedded in the lead close together. The exception is in countries where the plant material is often large with strong, thick stems, in which case the pins are better further apart. All pinholders should be rustproof. Pinholders of less than about 5 cm are of little use and 7 cm in diameter is the most useful and adaptable. Bigger sizes may be necessary in countries with larger plant material.

Placing stems

Slender stems cannot be supported by the pins but

▼ Pinholders support stems in an upright position or angled. Stems are impaled or slipped between the pins. Pinholders with wide-set pins are for holding Oasis.

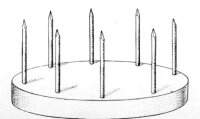

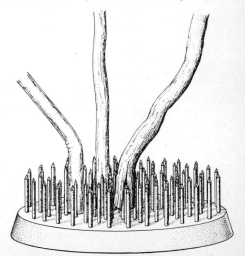

▲ Well-type pinholders can be bought ready-made, or improvised using a conventional pinholder in a food tin. Plasticine prevents pinholders from slipping.

they can be placed inside a larger, hollow stem which can itself be impaled on the pins. Pinholders can sometimes be found made especially for slender stems. They have fine pins placed closely together.

The stem ends of cut plant material should be pushed firmly down *on or between* the pins in an upright position. If a different angle is required the stem should be pressed gently into position after impaling.

Some woody stems are too hard for pushing directly on to the pins and should not be forced as this bends the pins. They can be prepared quite easily either by splitting the stem end, using a knife or flower scissors, or by cutting the end on a slant. Some very hard, woody stems are impaled easily when sharpened to a point with a knife.

Broad, soft stems such as hyacinth can be strengthened by inserting a small sturdy stick in the end. If the soft, outer stem splits it can be bound with wool. Hollow stems can have a stick inserted to give extra support.

In time pinholders become clogged with plant material; but they can be cleaned with a wire brush.

Securing pinholders

The weight of a heavy pinholder usually keeps it in position, but if it slips about and makes the placement of stems difficult, it can be held firmly with a compound product such as plasticine. There are other trade names for similar products, which vary in their adhesive quality. Many are sold especially for the use of flower arrangers. They are easier to apply when the container and pinholder are quite dry.

Using plasticine

Use small amounts rolled into blobs and pressed on to the base of the pinholder, or roll a larger amount into a sausage to place in a circle on the base. Press the pinholder down firmly and then twist it slightly to give good adhesion.

When you wish to remove the pinholder from the container, twist again and lift it up or lever it by using a blunt-ended knife.

Always be careful of your fingers when using a pinholder as the sharp pins can easily do some damage.

Plasticine can be cleaned off a pinholder by scraping it with a knife and then wiping with turpentine or a substitute for removing paint.

Pinholders in containers

Make sure that the container used is deep enough so that water covers the top of the pinholder, otherwise the stem ends will not receive water.

Well-type pinholders are also available. These are deep metal bowls, usually painted black or green, with built-in pins. Care should be taken to buy wells that hold plenty of water. These are excellent for use when supporting small amounts of plant material; for placing in

a pot-et-fleur (see p. 66); or for a concealed support behind a chunk of driftwood. A well-type pinholder is an economical container to use in conjunction with a base, in place of a decorative container. An inexpensive one can be made at home with a normal pinholder in a painted, lidless, empty food tin. It should have a broad base because it is not as heavy as the ready-made type.

Styles for pinholders

Pinholders do not hold as much plant material as blocks of Oasis and are better for sparse arrangements. It is not possible to place the stems to flow downwards, as with Oasis, unless the stems are themselves curved. For this reason most styles in pinholders tend to be upright.

Cover-ups

Various objects, either of plant material or of non-plant material, can be used to cover the mechanics.

When a deep container is used they are normally concealed by the sides of the container and are no problem. Plant material such as the broad flat leaves of geraniums, hostas, bergenias or ivy can be used to cover the Oasis if it stands above the rim of the container. They should be placed at an angle so that they lie flat against the foam. Leaves are sometimes used to hide a pinholder, although in a sparse design they tend to

▼ Mechanics can be concealed with plant material; and by windscreen glass, bark, or stones or pebbles.

give too much visual weight at the bottom. Many flower arrangers prefer to use objects such as pebbles, gravel, stones, coral or shells. These are natural materials and blend well because they are associated with plants. They also have interesting textures and lovely soft colouring. Shattered windscreen glass and marbles can also

be attractive, because they are not obtrusive in water.

The style of the arrangement should suggest the type of cover-up that is used.
1 Traditional designs using a lot of plant material, and probably arranged in wire-netting (see p. 45) or Oasis, usually have flat leaves to conceal the mechanics.
2 Landscape designs are

better when pebbles, stones, wood, shells or coral are used, depending on the type of landscape portrayed. This makes the design seem more naturalistic.
3 Modern designs can have polished pebbles or matt black stones or wood.
4 Abstract designs require experience in mechanics and cover-ups. They use a lot of space within the design, and both container and cover-up are obvious and so must be a part of the design. Inverted boxes and tins containing holes for stems may be used. Bases are often constructed with holes in them through which stems are impaled in a concealed container.

When to position cover-ups

Mechanics for traditional designs using many flowers and leaves and Oasis should be covered before the rest of the arrangement is begun — otherwise it becomes difficult to insert leaves. When placed in position first, concealing leaves can be lifted easily to insert flower stems. The result is that often less stems are needed in the arrangement.

In modern designs the cover-up is better placed in the design after the plant material and when the style and size of the design is evident. In abstract designs cover-ups should be worked out before the design starts.

▼ When attaching a candlecup to the top of a candlestick or similar container, provide support for plant material with a pinholder and Oasis.

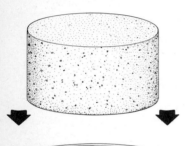

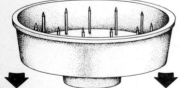

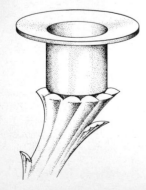

▲ A candlecup with pinholder and Oasis covered by 1-cm-mesh wire netting. Reel wire is used to tie the netting to the container.

Wire netting
Wire netting makes a useful support for stems. It can be used alone or with Oasis, a

pinholder, or both.

It can be bought from iron-mongers, hardware stores and garden centres. It comes in a variety of widths, but these are irrelevant because for flower arranging smaller pieces are cut off. It is sold by the yard or the metre. It is usual for flower arrangers to buy a metre of, say, 1-metre-wide netting. The wire can be cut with flower scissors if light, but heavier wire needs wire-cutters.

Mesh of about 5 cm diameter is useful for crumpling into deep containers such as urns to make a mound of irregularly spaced wires. A 2-cm mesh is used for a rigid cap, uncrumpled, as an extra support over Oasis. Mesh measuring 1 cm can be similarly used for smaller stems but is not wide enough for average stems.

Hardware cloth with square spaces is the most rigid and is not often used. Ship's netting is still stronger, with bigger holes, and is used in countries where there are larger plants and for really heavy driftwood and branches.

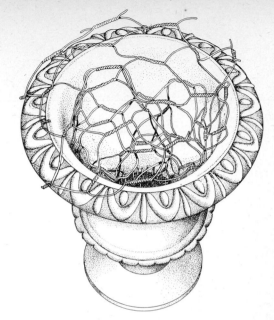

Netting with Oasis·

Cut a round, square or rectangle of 2-cm mesh to fit over the top and down the sides of the block of Oasis already placed in the container. Keep it as flat as possible, like a lid, and do not press it down too hard or it will cut into the foam. Secure the netting with one or more lengths of wire cut from a reel. Twist one end of a length to the netting at one side. Carry it around any stem on the container, handle, base or simply around the bottom. Take it up to the outer side and twist it on to the netting again. More than one length should be placed in different directions especially for a large arrangement. Using reel wire and netting results in the foam being held firmly in the container.

There are several advantages in these mechanics.
1 It is excellent when the Oasis block stands well out of the container and has little or no support from the container.
2 A large number of flowers placed in the front of a block of foam can cause it to break away. The netting, held well down with reel wire, prevents this and gives necessary stability when arrangements are used in churches

▲ In an urn or other deep container crumpled wire netting can be used, with a pinholder to provide extra support for heavy stems.

or for special events.
3 It gives extra support for branches whose weight can otherwise break the foam and cause them to fall out.
4 Beginners find it a useful second support because Oasis can become full of holes through the positions of stems being frequently changed.

Netting in a deep container
Five-cm mesh, crumpled, can be used to fill a deep container in place of Oasis. This enables stems to stand in deep water, which is considered by some people to lengthen the life of flowers,

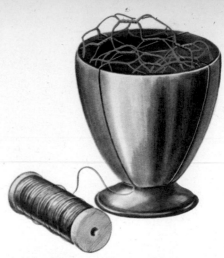

▲ Netting can be held down in a small container by rubber bands.

▲ Wire netting can be attached to some containers by reel wire wrapped round the container's stem, handles or base.

especially in hot countries, or when arrangements are required to last a longer time than usual. Two-cm mesh is too rigid for this purpose.

It is not as easy to position flowers in netting as in foam, and so arrangements can take longer to do.

Cut a piece that is as wide as the container's cavity and about three times its depth. Cavities vary in shape, and experience with your own containers is the best guide. The container should not be so crammed with wire that stems cannot be inserted but should be full enough to provide support.

Crumple up the wire so that some of the cut ends point upwards. These are useful for twisting round tall stems. Place the netting into the cavity so that it is full. Pull up some wire so that it stands about 4 cm above the rim of the container.

Some flower arrangers use only wire netting, crumpled, as a stem support; but accurate placement of stems can be very difficult. It is helped by the use of a pinholder in the bottom of the container, for the longer and heavier stems. These are pushed through the netting and on to the pins.

Securing stems

Netting can be very frustrating if it wobbles about while you are trying to arrange flowers. This problem can be solved in several ways:

1 If a pinholder is used in the bottom of the container the netting is anchored satisfactorily when the first stem is placed through it and on to the pins.

2 Lengths of reel wire or string can be attached either side of the netting and carried round the container's stem, handles or base in the

same way as described for the use of netting with Oasis.
3 When a small shallow bowl is used, two thick rubber bands can be used at right angles to hold down the netting.

Wire netting can soon become rusty and it is better dried after use. It should be replaced when it does become rusty because it is otherwise messy to use.

Pedestal arrangements

This is the term commonly used for larger designs placed on a construction that stands on the floor such as a marble, alabaster, wooden or metal pedestal, with a small shelf to hold a container on top. In some countries this style is called a 'mass'. The mechanics are not difficult, but more of them are necessary to support the greater number and weight of stems. There are several methods of support:

1 A deep urn can hold one or more large blocks of Oasis standing above the rim of the container.

2 Two-cm netting can be placed over the Oasis for extra stability, with reel wire attached in several places and carried around the container and the pedestal.

3 When a shallow container is used—and this is useful because it enables stems to be placed to flow gracefully downwards—wire netting as a second support is essential. It must be secured with reel wire carried around the pedestal, otherwise the Oasis can tip out of the shallow container.

4 Wire netting can be used crumpled in a deep container when deep water is preferred. A pinholder is necessary in the bottom to support the longest stems, and some netting should stand about 10 cm above the container's rim to give extra support.

When a pedestal is used for a function where there are many people passing by, it is advisable to wire or string it to a permanent and stable part of the room's furnishings such as a pillar, pew end or screen, or a nail in the wall or skirting, so that it cannot be knocked over.

▶ An economical pedestal arrangement of shrub foliage with a few chrysanthemums, by Dorothy Haworth. The arrangement is made in two blocks of Oasis in a low bowl covered with a cap of netting, which is tied to the pedestal with reel wire.

Driftwood

Weathered wood for use in flower arrangements can include many items besides driftwood, although this is the name generally given to all such material. Every shape can be used, according to its intended purpose. This can range from concealing mechanics to augmenting a theme or a shape, or acting as the main feature of an arrangement.

Wood weathered by the elements is referred to as driftwood although it may not have been in the sea at any time. It includes roots, parts of tree trunks, leafless branches, stumps, woody stems and unidentifiable chunks of wood. It is plant material in the same way as flowers and leaves, but it is unique in that two pieces never look quite the same. This is the fascination. It is also ageless and can be kept indefinitely. It can be found in wooded areas whether by the sea or in the country, especially after storms. Sometimes it is sold by florists, garden centres and flower clubs. The colour varies according to the type of wood and the time it has been exposed to the elements. Wood that has stood in strong sun becomes bleached grey or white. Textures of wood also vary from smooth to very rough, and there are many shapes.

Uses of driftwood
Large shapes can be mounted like sculpture.

Smaller pieces may be used to hide mechanics.

Cross-cuts of trunks make good bases.

Branches provide lines in design.

Chunks of various sizes can be used in front of or behind flowers and leaves.

Containers can be made from suitable pieces.

Choice
Soft wood is not worth collecting. It soon rots and disintegrates. Look for hard

▼ Driftwood needs preparation. Clean it (**1**) with a small knife and a wire brush. To secure it, plaster of Paris may be suitable (**2**), or (**3**) a base with an upright screw, or (**4**) a peg leg extension.

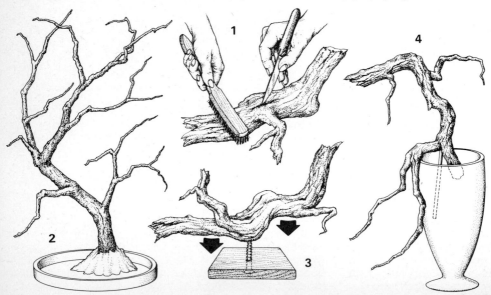

wood or wood that has few soft parts.

Cleaning

Wood suits most homes if it is clean and, sometimes, polished. All wood needs washing before taking indoors. Scrub dirty wood in water containing detergent, but avoid scrubbing grey wood because the greyness is only on the surface and can soon disappear. Disinfectant and insecticide may be necessary if the wood is infested. Dry, after washing, in sunshine or a warm place.

Grooming

Most wood has small crevices containing soft wood. There can also be peeling bark and broken branches that need cutting off. Use a pointed knife to remove soft wood. Trim away broken ends with secateurs and scrape off loose bark with a knife. If you prefer branches and stems stripped of bark it is more easily removed if first soaked for several days.

Shaping

Few pieces of wood can be found with perfect shape, and most need modification. Study the shape as found from all angles. Then decide, without hurry, which parts need removing. Large sections can be sawn off but avoid major cuts if possible because an unsightly scar can be left. Two or more pieces of wood of the same type and colour can be joined together to make a larger piece, using a reliable wood adhesive.

▶ Driftwood supported by a peg leg in a stoneware container, with reedmace repeating the pattern and dahlias for emphasis; arranged by the author.

Polishing and colouring

After shaping decide whether polish and a change of colour would improve the wood. Do not polish grey wood unless you wish to lose the greyness. Other colours can be brushed with a wire brush to give a soft sheen, rubbed with sandpaper or sanded with a machine. Shoe or furniture wax gives a soft sheen if used liberally. Coloured polish alters the colour. Wood can also be stained and varnished for protection with matt or shiny lacquer. Linseed oil darkens and protects but does not colour or polish. Bleach gives a yellowish, paler colour. Wood can also be painted with emulsion or oil-based paint.

Supports

1 A peg leg is often a help in holding wood firmly in position. Drill a hole wherever support is needed and insert a length of wood, preferably of similar colour and type. Secure it with adhesive.
2 A screw, or more than one, can be positioned through a wooden base from the bottom and up into the driftwood.
3 A pinholder and Oasis can support slender branches.
4 Wood clamps can be bought but should be hidden in the finished arrangement.

5 Plaster of Paris can be used for heavier branches and chunks. Mix the powder with water to a stiff paste and quickly mound it up and insert the wood at the required angle. Hold it for a few minutes until the plaster sets. The wood can also be set in a tin or can with plaster of Paris, Polyfilla or a similar compound. The plaster and the tin should be painted so that they are not obtrusive. This type of support is permanent.

Styles

When wood is used in an arrangement it is better to use little plant material, otherwise it is hidden.

Design

Once you have collected a small stock of containers, mechanics and equipment and have learnt how to condition and support plant material it is helpful to learn more about design. This word implies sophisticated knowledge but it simply means 'putting in order', something we do most days when we tidy our living rooms and offices. When at the same time as tidying we also try to display things attractively, such as ornaments on a shelf and furniture in a room, we can be said to be 'designing'. The first step in this process is selection. Objects are chosen to be placed together that appear to have some relationship, and bearing in mind their size, colour, shape, texture—and, sometimes, their associations.

SIZE

It is easy to recognize when an ornament is too big for a shelf, a cupboard too large for a room, a hat too big for a small lady. In the same way small flowers are not suitable for a large container, and large flowers look too big in a small container.

When objects placed together are not too far apart in size, they are said to be 'in scale'. Scale is relative and an object by itself is not large or small until it is seen near another object. For example a baby elephant looks big until it is seen next to its mother.

Flowers and leaves used together in an arrangement usually look better when they are closely related in size. For example a snowdrop is too small to combine with a large parrot tulip and would look better arranged with a primrose.

A flower arrangement is made up of many parts: a container; sometimes a base; flowers; leaves; and sometimes other plant material. All these parts should be close in size, otherwise if there is a big difference between them one component tends to look huge and the others seem dwarfed.

Choosing sizes

When selecting the components you can begin with the flowers or with the container; but in either case the sizes of each should be

▼ From left to right: the container is too big for the plant material; the flower is too big for the container; flower, leaf and container are in scale.

related. When you buy or pick flowers think of the containers you own. If you have no large containers avoid buying large flowers. If you have large rooms, larger flowers and containers will look better. Try to think of 'scale' during the time of selection:

1 Each piece of plant material should be close in size which means that the chosen leaves should not be much bigger than the flowers.

2 The container should suit the size of the flowers and leaves.

3 The base should not dwarf the container and plant material. Too big a base is a common fault.

4 The whole design, including the base, should be 'in scale' with its setting. A big civic hall needs large arrangements. A hospital bedside table needs a small design.

Some flower arrangements need more attention to scale than others: ·

1 Miniatures are tiny arrangements usually no more than about 10 cm overall. The plant material and container should be in scale but scaled down. A thimble or bottle cap could be used for a container, and tiny rock plants for flowers.

In a photograph when there is no indication of size a miniature arrangement looks like an average-sized design if it is correctly scaled.

2 An arrangement on a tall pedestal or a large mass design needs bigger plant material, such as palm leaves, tall delphiniums,

the biggest dahlias or hydrangeas.

3 Landscapes which are designs in naturalistic style (see p. 58), should repeat the natural scale. If a figurine of an animal is used it should be in the same scale with the plant material as it would be in life. For example a model of a deer is not in correct scale when used with daffodils. It would look better in this case if flowers were omitted and a twig represented a tree—in scale.

Proportion

Although each flower and leaf may be well chosen and in scale with the container, an arrangement can have too many flowers in it, so that the container looks overwhelmed with them. This is a case of 'too much', not too little or too big. Scale concerns relative sizes but proportion concerns relative *amounts*. The flowers are out of proportion when a small container is stuffed full of them. However in Victorian times there were many overcrowded designs —in our eyes—because people's sense of proportion was different from ours.

Large designs still tend to be over-stuffed with plant material and they usually look better when only a few pieces of material which is large in scale are used.

49

SHAPE

There are many shapes in flowers, leaves, fruits and wood. This can make it difficult to choose those that look best when combined in a flower arrangement, and some kind of guide can help make this easier. Plant material can, generally speaking, be classed into three shape groups.

1 Elongated shapes

These are called 'line' in design terms. They make the eye travel along rather than holding it in one position. Lines vary in size and type, and may be thin or thick, wavy or straight, simple or complicated. Their common characteristic is that they move the eye. In plant material they include branches; spikey flowers such as delphiniums; leaves like iris; grasses; and bulrushes. Lines give activity and movement to a design.

2 Round shapes

Round or nearly round shapes are called 'points' in design terms. They hold the eye momentarily in the same way as traffic lights, people's eyes, stars and the centre of a dart board. One's eyes are at once attracted to points.

Many flowers are round in shape, being either spherical, like a hydrangea, or flat like a daisy, which has another 'point' in its centre. Fruit such as apples and oranges are points, and berries, though smaller and all clustered together, are each a point.

Points are such dominant shapes that they are usually better used in small quantities.

3 In-between shapes

Some plant material has shapes that cannot be defined clearly as round or elongated. They are trans-

◄ In plants, elongated shapes include ivy trails, delphinium flowers, prunus and any leafless branches and iris leaves.

► Round and nearly round shapes: hippeastrum, chrysanthemum and double narcissi.

◄ Shapes in between round and elongated include leaves of hosta, laurel and rhododendron.

itional shapes which partially move the eye, but not as strongly as lines; and they almost hold the eye, but not as strongly as points.

Selection

There are several ways of combining shapes in a design. Often it is satisfying to the eye to see some of each:
1 One type of plant material forming a line, such as long branches or leaves, to move the eye in a design and give activity and rhythm.
2 A few rounded shapes such as open roses, dahlias or daisy flowers to hold the eye and act as 'stars'—the most important feature of the design.
3 In-between shapes, usually leaves, to soften the contrast between the lines and the rounds.

In shopping for flowers or picking them in the garden, it is helpful when selecting from the wealth of plant material often available to think of it in terms of lines, rounds and in-between shapes, and to choose one of each type for an arrangement. With experience, you can also experiment with other differing combinations.

Designs of one shape

There are no rules about the use of shapes, and arrangements can be made of one, two or all three shapes according to the effect you wish to achieve and the available plant material. Designs can be made entirely of leaves with an in-between shape, or with all rounds such as fruit, giving a more static design, or of all lines such as an arrangement of branches which gives an active effect. Most satisfying to the eye, however, is usually a combination of all three.

▼ Arrangements can incorporate either one or several types of shape.

COLOUR

This is one of the dominant and enjoyable qualities in flowers. The colours combined in a single flower and their relative areas can be a source of ideas for colour schemes in flower arrangements, and inspiration can also be found in the same way from such things as shells, birds, scenery, weather and paintings. The more you experiment with colours the more skilled you become in selection.

Colours have an expressive quality which can evoke an atmosphere. Shades can look gloomy, tones subtle, tints can appear young and pretty, bright colours gay. This knowledge is useful for interpretive arrangements in flower shows. Colour also has associations, such as red and green with Christmas or blue with the sea, according to personal experience.

The intensity of colours may be weak or strong. Weaker colours are neutralized and are useful for containers, bases and backgrounds for flowers. They enhance, and do not vie with, the flowers' brilliant colourings. Small areas of bright blues are often more acceptable than large areas because pure colour is more exciting and tiring.

Colours appear light or heavy according to the amount of white and black present. Unequal weights are usually best together. Colours can also give an effect of movement. Yellow lifts, orange and red advance, blue and violet recede.

Surroundings and colour

Colours change according to the lighting, and other colours that surround them. They can appear darker or lighter, brilliant or dull or even change hue.

The spectrum

Daylight (white light) combines the colours of the spectrum. When we see colour it is the one colour which is reflected that we see, while the others are absorbed.

Light values

The amount of colour reflected (the luminosity) depends on the light value of the colour. The proportions of the colour circle show the relative luminosity of the spectrum colours. In dimmer lighting the more luminous colours should be used.

Colour temperature

Colours have qualities which suggest warmth or coolness. Warmth is generally associated with reds and oranges, coolness with blues and greens. The aesthetic and subjective qualities of colour and temperature are very important in flower arranging.

A colour circle helps show colour relationships. Innumerable combinations are possible of hue, value (tint, shade, tone), intensity (strength) and texture. From the centre each segment here shows: tints, tone, hue, shades.

Hue One colour as distinct from another. There are six basic hues: red, orange, yellow, green, blue, violet.

Tint A hue with white added.

Shade A hue with black added.

Tone A hue with grey (black and white) added.

1 Monochromatic colouring is tints, shades and tones of one colour. Plant material is rarely one coloured, but one colour often predominates.

2 Adjacent colouring is the use of two to four colours adjacent to each other, and closely related, on the colour circle.

3 Complementary colouring is the use of colours opposite, or approximately opposite, each other on the colour circle.

4 Triadic colouring uses three colours equidistant on the colour circle. The best such schemes tend to use colours of unequal strength.

53

TEXTURE

The surfaces of all objects have some type of texture. It is a 'feel' quality. Present-day designers are especially interested in textural effects, in architecture, furnishings and embroidery. Young children touch many things to see how they feel. Later the appearance of objects tells us how they feel without touching, although we may still enjoy touching sleek, fluffy, smooth and downy surfaces.

The look and feel of an object, however, are not always the same; there is a difference between *actual* and *visual* texture because of the way objects, such as flower petals, are grouped. A poppy looks and feels sleek but a carnation feels sleek and looks rough.

Flower arrangers are concerned with visual texture because designs are made to look at, not to touch as some sculpture.

Broadly, textures fit into two categories, rough and smooth. Within these two groups are many variations, especially in plant material, which is rich in textures of every description. There are fluffy grasses, sticky buds, shiny leaves, downy fruits, velvety petals, prickly stems, sleek wood, rough seed-heads and many more. Although not such a dominant quality as colour, texture gives great interest to flower arrangements, but usually because of *contrasts* rather than similarities. Some arrangements need even more textural interest than others, to avoid monotony:

1 Dried plant material is less strong in colour interest and includes many rough surfaces. It needs smooth containers and leaves for contrast.
2 Fruit and vegetables are often solid in form and textural contrasts add relief.
3 Arrangements of predominatingly one colour need the interest of textural contrasts.
4 Modern designs with fewer flowers and leaves

▼ Some textures of plant material. From top left to right: globe artichoke seeds; prickly *Agave americana* 'Marginata'; *Corylus maxima* 'Purpurea'; and a pine cone.

◀ Arum lilies and peeled ivy stems arranged by Edith Brack in a stoneware container. Space is used within the design.

▲ A traditional mass arrangement by Julia Clements, with a solid outline and using little space within the design.

look more dramatic when textures are very different.

Texture is closely related to colour and can alter its appearance. A visually rough-textured carnation looks darker than a smooth poppy although they may be the same colour of red.

SPACE

It is a matter of choice how much space you include within a grouping of plant material, and it greatly alters the effect. Flower arrangements can be solid in appearance, with flowers and leaves placed closely together, which emphasizes the outline, or spacious, which emphasizes the individual shapes of the flowers and leaves and their textural qualities.

A solid cone uses no space between the flowers and leaves. Traditional arrangements, though looser than a cone, use little space within the design. Modern arrangements tend to use more space because this gives a greater sense of order, and more emphasis to single objects, and is in keeping with the present-day regard for space in our surroundings. Space is considered as a working quality by modern designers in the same way account is taken of colour, texture and shape.

Surrounding space
The space in which an arrangement stands also needs consideration. If a design is too big for its boundaries, such as a niche or walls and windows, there is an appearance of overcrowding. There should be a pleasing relationship between the design and its framework.

Pedestal-type containers, trivets and stands are popular at present because they provide space below an arrangement, which gives a light effect and allows the lower plant material to be seen well.

BALANCE

A flower arrangement can fall over because it is unstable; it can also look as though it could fall over, or merely appear lop-sided or top or bottom heavy. It then lacks visual balance. Some objects attract our eyes more quickly than others; when incorrectly placed within the design they disturb our sense of balance.

Our eyes tend to relate to an imaginary *vertical*. line bisecting the container; so a lop-sided effect is given by too much eye-attracting plant material placed on one side. Good balance is achieved when the eye is equally attracted to either side, whether with similar or different objects.

A symmetrically shaped design such as a triangle or a circle is easy to balance because the outline shapes on either side can be made similar. When flowers are arranged asymmetrically these shapes are not the same, but plant material that attracts the eye equally is placed either side of the imaginary vertical line in the centre.

Good balance is also needed either side of an imaginary *horizontal* line going through the centre of the complete design. A big base may attract the eye too much to the bottom part of the arrangement. Big flowers, unbalanced by anything lower down, may give top-heaviness. Most people have a fair sense of balance, and correction is easy if you remove or add eye-attracting material as necessary.

◄ The large yellow dahlia has more eye-pull than the daisy below it because of its size.

► Objects of identical size and shape can differ in emphasis if one is more brightly coloured.

◄ A round shape, like a marigold flower, is more emphatic than a long shape such as a red-hot poker flower.

EMPHASIS

Some objects attract the eye more quickly than others; for example a larger sculpture will do so rather than a smaller one. In plant material, too, certain characteristics attract more attention than others. These qualities closely associated with balance can be used to provide emphasis, because when making an arrangement the design is more pleasing to look at if some flowers or leaves are more important than others. The same principle is used in other works of art; certain areas of a painting are emphasized, others are less important; and in a book or a film some of the characters are of greater significance than others. Usually only a few such objects or characters are needed, but far more objects of less importance.

In a flower arrangement a better design is achieved combining two or three larger flowers with many smaller ones and/or leaves than when all large flowers are used.

Flower arrangers refer to the dominant part of a design as the centre of interest' or 'the focal point'. It simply means the main feature. It is usually made from larger flowers, brighter colours, shinier textures, solid forms, rounder shapes and sometimes, in modern designs, from enclosed spaces.

Care needs to be taken over the positioning of the most important features because otherwise the balance of the design can be upset. For example when larger flowers are put on one side of an arrangement and smaller ones on the other the effect is lop-sided. A central position, though unadventurous, is usually safe when beginning flower arranging.

In traditional designs the centre of interest is placed in the centre or just below the centre of the complete design, including the base and container. In a modern arrangement it can go anywhere as long as the result appears balanced. In the abstract style there is usually more than one centre of interest. These are called emphasis points and are equated through the design to lead the eye around it.

Although the centre of interest is an important feature it should not be such a 'bull's eye' that your atten-tion has difficulty in leaving it. For this reason it is better not to have a big difference in size between the largest and the smallest flowers.

In terms of style flower arrangements can be broadly classified into those with, and those without, space in the design (or 'line arrangements' and 'mass arrangements'). In some countries hybrids with a strong line but also a mass of plant material are called 'mass-line' or 'line-mass'. Most period designs are mass, with the exception of oriental arrangements. Many modern ones are line.

▼ Larger round flowers are useful to provide emphasis in the centre of a solid design.

▼ Large flowers at the top of the arrangement balance the container and large oval leaves.

Styles of arrange-ment

The term 'style' refers to the manner in which plant material is assembled. It is a general classification. Some designs are hybrids, others have no recognizable style and some are highly individualistic. Style in any aspect of design is influenced by other arts, culture, social conditions and new materials. It is often more obvious in retrospect.

LANDSCAPES

Landscape styles are the most naturalistic of any designs. They were first made in China many years ago. The term refers to scenery and not to shape. Plant material and objects from a scene are arranged to evoke its atmosphere. Restraint, here, is usually the secret of success. A lakeside landscape could include bulrushes, grasses, reeds and water-iris flowers with stones or driftwood to conceal the mechanics, all in a low bowl featuring water.

TRIANGULAR STYLES

This popular classical design is triangular only in silhouette. It needs a stemmed container to appear to advantage. The mechanics can be Oasis standing above the rim, with or without netting, or netting pulled above the rim, used with a pinholder. Triangles should include: line plant material; plain flat leaves; rounded flowers or a rosette of leaves; and smaller flowers and leaves.

There are no rules for assembling any arrangements.

◄ Spring landscape by Marian Aaronson of corkscrew hazel, fungi and daffodils.

◀ A triangular arrangement by Richard Jeffery. The tall container enables the lower stems to be seen.

1

2

Many people find it easier, however, to use the following method for a triangle. Place a straight stem about twice the container's height (according to the stem's dimensions) two thirds of the way back; and place stems either side to complete the tips of the triangle and two shorter stems facing forward in front and towards the back for depth (right, **1**). Add plain leaves to hide the mechanics, and place emphasis flowers or a rosette of leaves centrally (**2**). Use extra plant material for the desired full or sparse effect, keeping within a triangular silhouette (**3**). A sense of radiation is achieved when stem ends appear to meet at a central point. Curved lower stems give a softer effect and need not be the same plant material as the backbone.

3

CIRCULAR DESIGNS

A posy or circular style is a traditional and natural way to present flowers. Nosegays were carried originally as a precaution against infection and often included sweet-smelling herbs. They are presented in some ceremonies even today. Early Victorian posies or tussie-mussies were placed in wrought metal, porcelain or mother-of-pearl holders lined with moss. They were carried but had a chain linked to the wearer's belt to free the hands. Often the flowers were arranged in rings of colour bound with raffia around a single rose bud, giving a slightly domed effect. A finish of leaves and a lace frill surrounded them.

Throughout history the rounded bouquet has been the style of Europe. Only in the twentieth century did a mass design become more often a triangle.

Modern versions

The container can be low or tall. For a dinner-table arrangement it could be a foam-holding saucer for a low bowl. The mechanics can be Oasis, capped or not by wire netting, or crumpled netting with or without a pinholder.

Cover the mechanics with flat leaves (below, **1**).

Add flowers facing in all directions to form the outline of a whole or half sphere (**2**). Then fill the centre. Round flowers are easier to use than spiky ones (**3**).

1

2

3

◀ This circular, traditional posy style originated in Europe. It is too tall for a table centre at a seated meal; but could be displayed on a side table.

▶ A back-to-front 'S' shape can be traced through the gentle curves of this design by Jane Derbyshire.

1

2

3

THE HOGARTH CURVE

William Hogarth (1697–1764) was an English illustrator, engraver and painter who named the irregular but rhythmic movement of an 'S' curve 'the line of beauty'. It has since been re-named the 'Hogarth curve'. Various interpretations have evolved in flower arrangement including a soft swirling curve, a stiffer sharper curve and a back-to-front 'S' shape.

Curved plant material looks especially attractive arranged in this latter way. The container must be tall, to allow a downward sweep. The mechanics should be Oasis, placed above its rim. Plant material should include: curved lines, because straight lines will not make the shape; plain leaves for concealing mechanics; emphasis plant material; and supporting smaller leaves and/or flowers to fill in if wished.

Method

Place the upward-curving stem on the top of the Oasis but to one side with the tip curving inwards. The lower curve also curves inwards but is placed opposite in the side part of the block (left, **1**). Further plant material should follow these lines, all meeting at a central point where leaves are used for concealing mechanics (**2**), and emphasis material is placed.

61

◄ A crescent of spring flowers in green and white arranged by Joan Ewing.

need: a number of curved stems which move in both directions; plain leaves for concealing the Oasis; emphasis flowers, leaves or fruit; and plant material for filling in, if a more compact shape is wanted.

Method

For a crescent similar to the illustration, place curved stems at either side of the Oasis (**1**). Add leaves to cover the Oasis (**2**). Fill in with other plant material to follow the crescent shape (**3**).

A horizontal crescent

Crescents similar to the illustration can be made in a tall container, candlestick or bottle. A candlecup is necessary in the top. It is also an attractive style when arranged in a low container placed in a high position such as a shelf, mantlepiece, church screen or lecturn. Wherever a horizontal crescent is placed there must be space below for the stems to trail gracefully downwards.

CRESCENT ARRANGEMENTS

A crescent is a graceful style which can be made in a variety of ways. It can be placed upright in the shape of a new moon or face downwards with a more trailing effect. It can be used for a table arrangement as a change from the posy shape.

Mechanics

A crescent can be made in Oasis or on a pinholder, but wire netting is more difficult to use since stem placement is not precise.

Plant material

Curved stems are essential, because straight lines will not give the shape. You will

1   2   3

► Fruit can make an economical arrangement. This design is by Julia Clements.

An upright crescent

This can be made in a low or a tall container by placing a long, curved, upright stem in the centre of one side of the Oasis, curving upwards and inwards at the top. Place a second main stem on the other side of the Oasis in the same way but in the opposite direction. Cover the Oasis with leaves and add further plant material following the original lines and leaving space in the centre to form a crescent.

A crescent on a table

This can be made in Oasis, horizontally or upright, in a low container with emphasis flowers in the centre.

DESIGNING WITH FRUIT

Fruit can be combined in arrangements with flowers, leaves or preserved and dried plant material. It looks festive at celebration times such as Christmas. It is easy to position in Oasis but lasts longer when arranged without wet mechanics, which can turn fruit mouldy.

Mechanics

Wooden meat-skewers and lengths of dowel (round sticks from a DIY shop) can be used for impaling the fruit into Oasis or into another piece of fruit for support. If the skewer is washed beforehand the fruit will remain clean to eat: wires damage fruit.

Grapes can be attached to a skewer by means of a wire twisted round the stem. A pineapple is heavy and is usually better centred. It needs at least two skewers pushed into the base to give support.

Fruit normally looks better when arranged in groups of each kind and colour. It is good to vary textures. Larger shapes can be placed in the centre, and smaller and more elongated shapes at the sides, to give an effect of tapering size. A few sprigs of fresh foliage can be pushed into the Oasis to soften the shapes. When this is not used, preserved foliage (see pp. 67-9) can be inserted instead.

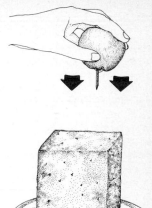

▲ Fruit can be impaled on a wooden skewer, cocktail stick or dowel for placing in Oasis or other mechanics.

MODERN ARRANGEMENTS

The modern style, which is sometimes called free-style or free-form (this simply means free of the geometric form of a triangle, crescent, Hogarth curve or circle), is assembled quite differently from traditional styles. It does not depend on a preconceived framework which is filled in, and there is no visualized outline. The design builds up as you arrange the pieces of plant material, chosen for their interest and for contrasting forms, textures and colours. Eye-attracting plant material is assembled either side of imaginary horizontal and vertical axis lines using plenty of space within the design.

Choose a container which is simple and modern in style; and plant material with contrasting shape and texture which is in scale with the container and with itself. Try to have several shapes and textures in plant material to choose from as you work.

Use a pinholder if possible. It does not need as much hiding as Oasis or wire netting and the design is kept simple.

Place one piece of plant material such as a branch to one side of the container to unbalance it (below; **1**). Add a piece of dissimilar plant material on the other side (**2**) and strengthen these placements (**3**). You should feel by now that you have equal eye-pull either side of the imaginary axis. If not, add plant material until you once again feel that the arrangement is balanced. The plant material can be similar or dissimilar. Continue to balance and unbalance as the arrangement builds up, until you feel the design is complete.

Central placements do not affect the balance. Plant material for emphasis can be placed anywhere—at the top, in the centre or at the sides, as long as the final design seems balanced.

Make sure that there is space within the design so that each piece of plant material is clearly seen.

The container

This is an important choice in achieving a good modern design. Its shape, texture and colour are a more obvious part of the design than in a traditional arrangement, where the container is partially hidden by the plant material. Modern stoneware and pottery in simple shapes with interesting texture and earthy colours are best.

The mechanics

In modern designs these should be simple. It is better to use a pinholder whenever possible because it is easily concealed, unlike Oasis with netting, which needs plant material to hide it and so tends to spoil the clear-cut design needed for a successful modern style.

▶ A free-form design, by the author, of chrysanthemums, bergenia leaves and branches of geweiholtz.

1

2

3

POT-ET-FLEUR

A pot-et-fleur is a decoration that combines plants and cut flowers. The plants can be grown permanently and the flowers can be added from time to time. In this way your home or office displays something fresh and green at all times. This style is especially useful for people who have exceptionally busy periods at times or who are frequently away from home.

First find a deep container with room enough for the roots of plants. An old Victorian wash bowl, garden urns or copper pans are suitable and there are many simple, modern forms in pottery bowls.

Buy two or three plants that are easy to grow and which suit the same conditions of light and moisture.

Advice about this should be available from the shop or garden centre selling them.

At the same time buy a small bag of John Innes compost No. 2 or a similar compost for houseplants, a small packet of charcoal and a few handfuls of gravel. A builder's yard can supply this if the garden centre cannot.

Method

Place a 2-to-4-cm layer of gravel in the bottom of the container: plant roots should not stand in water, and the gravel will provide drainage. Then sprinkle charcoal over the top to keep the water sweet, and add a layer of compost.

Turn the plants out of their pots. Plastic pots can be squeezed to loosen the soil. Pottery may need to be turned upside down and knocked on a table edge. This loosens the plant, which should fall into your hand. Avoid watering the plant before doing this, otherwise the soil may fall off the roots. Arrange the plants in the bowl and fill the gaps between with compost, firming it well down with your hands. The soil should not cover the previous soil level of the plants. At least 2 cm should be left above the soil level and below the rim of the container to enable the compost to be watered without spillage.

Sink a darkly painted tin, or plastic bowl, containing a pinholder, in the centre of the compost to hold cut flowers.

cut flowers

compost
charcoal
gravel

Preserving with glycerine

Whether you arrange flowers often or infrequently a stock of glycerined foliage is invaluable. Preserved leaves can be arranged with fresh or dried flowers, or by themselves in a permanent display. They are an excellent and ready-to-hand substitute for fresh foliage when climate or expense makes it scarce.

The process

Buy a bottle of glycerine from a chemist or drug store. Pour the contents into a jar and fill the bottle twice over with hot water, adding it to the glycerine and stirring. Stand branches in the solution, splitting and scraping woody stems first. Remove damaged leaves so that they do not waste glycerine. Keep the glycerine mixture in the jar topped up to prevent the stem ends from drying out. Left-over glycerine can be used again.

Single leaves can be submerged in a bowl of the solution. Leaves which take a long time to absorb the solution should be mopped with it all over before the stem end is placed in the jar.

When is a leaf preserved?

Timing by days is uncertain. It is easier to tell by the change of colour. A preserved leaf changes colour from green to a shade of brown as the glycerine replaces the water in the cells. If beads of glycerine appear on the surface of leaves with thin tissue, remove the branches and wipe the leaves with tissues. They can also

MATERIAL TO PRESERVE WITH GLYCERINE

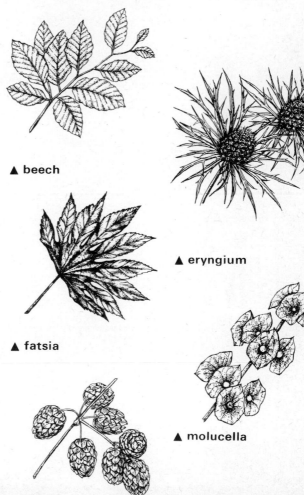

▲ beech

▲ eryngium

▲ fatsia

▲ molucella

▲ hops

Pour glycerine into a jam jar.

Add twice the quantity of hot water.

Remove damaged and crowded leaves. Split stem ends.

Stand stems in the solution.

Types of plant material
Try all kinds of plant material. You should find that many leaves can be preserved with glycerine, but few flowers.

be washed in detergent and water.

No glycerine is wasted if the plant material wilts before taking it up. Treat only mature foliage, as young leaves wilt quickly. Leaves beginning to turn colour in autumn will not preserve because they have ceased

to take up moisture of any kind. In Europe July and August are usually good months for preserving; whatever the country or month of the year, however, the secret is to use leaves that are mature but not old.

▲ Fatsia leaves submerged in a solution of glycerine and water.

Storage
Store preserved plant material in a dry place, otherwise it becomes mildewed. It should not be kept in a plastic bag—a cardboard box is better.

Colours
The colours vary from rich brown and almost black to light tan and cream. Lighter effects can be achieved by standing the leaves in strong sunlight after preservation is completed.

Uses in arrangements
No water is needed, but preserved plant material can be placed in Oasis or water without harm if it is well dried in between use. Alternatively it can have the stem ends dipped into melted wax or nail varnish to seal them. Most leaves last for years and remain supple and tough, but beech may have to be preserved every year or two if it is used in a dry room.

▶ Larger leaves such as aspidistra should first be mopped with glycerine-and-water solution.

SUITABLE FOLIAGE TO PRESERVE WITH GLYCERINE

Foliage	Weeks	Comment
aspidistra	12	mop; beige in colour
atriplex	$\frac{1}{2}$	beige
beech	1—2	green beech more successful
bergenia	3—4	immerse
box	3—4	beige
broom	2	almost black
camellia	4	dark brown
choisya	3	light beige
cotoneaster	2—4	colour varies with type
elaeagnus	4—6	variegation is lost
fatsia	2—6	mop or submerge
ferns	2	pick when spores show
grevillea	2	colour varies
ivy	2—3	mop or submerge
hellebore	2—3	light brown
laurel	2—3	very tough; dark brown
magnolia	3—4	tough; dark brown
mahonia	2—3	medium brown
oak	2	light brown
pittosporum	2	medium brown
rhododendron	2	single leaves better
rose	2	use woody stem; dark green
rubber plant	4	mop or submerge
Solomon's seal	1—2	treat after flowering
spotted laurel	3	variegation lost; dark brown
sweet chestnut	1—2	single leaves better
whitebeam	2	brown with grey underside

Other plant material to try includes hydrangea flowers, iris seed-pods, old man's beard and pussy willow catkins, which take about two weeks to process; lime flowers stripped of leaves; and teasels, which take about three weeks. Weather, date of picking and temperature can influence the time taken.

Drying plant material

The difference between drying plant material and preserving it in glycerine is that drying involves removing all moisture. After the process is completed, rather than any substance having been added or replaced, the plant material is quite dehydrated.

There are three basic methods of drying plant material, which can all be used at home.
1 Air-drying.
2 The use of desiccants.
3 Pressing.
Vacuum freeze-drying is also practised but it needs sophisticated equipment.

The selection of plant material is the same whatever the method. Pick plant material on a dry day so that subsequent drying indoors is quick and colour retention is better. Most flowers should be gathered just before they are fully mature. Pick seedheads before they become weather damaged. Select only good specimens and remove any damaged leaves or flowers, and choose plant material for air-drying that has rigid or strong tissue.

AIR-DRYING

This is a common method and easy to use. All that is necessary is for the plant material to be surrounded by dry air for a matter of days.

Remove the leaves as these do not dry successfully. Tie the stem ends together using string or a rubber band. Make the bunches small and spread out the flower heads so that the air reaches them. Hang the bunches upside down to pre-vent the 'necks' from shrivelling before drying is completed.

Leave for a few days, until the plant material feels crisp and dry to touch, before storing.

Places for drying

Bunches can be hung in the airing cupboard, in a dry spare room or near a boiler; sometimes a garage or outhouse may be dry enough. They can be hung on a coathanger, or on a clothes airer if there are many bunches.

Drying in water

Hydrangea, bells of Ireland and heather dry more successfully if they are placed with the stem ends in about 2 cm of water. They should be mature before picking.

Storing

Dried plant material needs careful storing because it tends to be fragile. Wrap it in tissue paper in cardboard boxes or leave it hanging in bunches. A dark place is advisable because bright light fades the colours. When it is arranged, strong light should also be avoided. Plastic bags should not be used for storage as they encourage mildew. Dried plant material should never be placed in a damp atmos-

SOME SUITABLE PLANTS FOR AIR-DRYING

Flowers
acanthus
acroclinium
delphinium
echinops
eryngium
globe artichoke
heather
helichrysum
helipterum
larkspur
lavender
love-lies-bleeding
pearly everlasting
pussy willow
statice
yarrow

Seedheads
allium
angelica
bulrush
Chinese lantern
clematis
cow parsley
dock
honesty
iris
love-in-a-mist
pampas grass
oriental poppy
peony
rushes, cereals, grasses, sedges
sunflowers
teasel
verbascum

phere because it can re-absorb moisture and then it flops. There are just a few varieties that dry permanently and do not take up moisture again, including achillea (yarrow), teasels and grasses.

Re-shaping

Dried plant material can become flattened during storage. Re-shape it by holding for a few seconds in the steam of a boiling kettle; and then stroke the material back to shape. If necessary, use tissues to pad out hollow shapes until they are dry.

THE USE OF DESICCANTS

Desiccants are substances which absorb and retain water. Plant material can be buried in them for varying lengths of time. The natural form shrinks only slightly and the colour retention is good. It is the most suitable method for single flowers, such as roses, peonies, marigolds and dahlias, which do not respond to air-drying. The results are fragile and need great care when handled, which makes them impractical for many people. Desiccants include silica gel, alum,

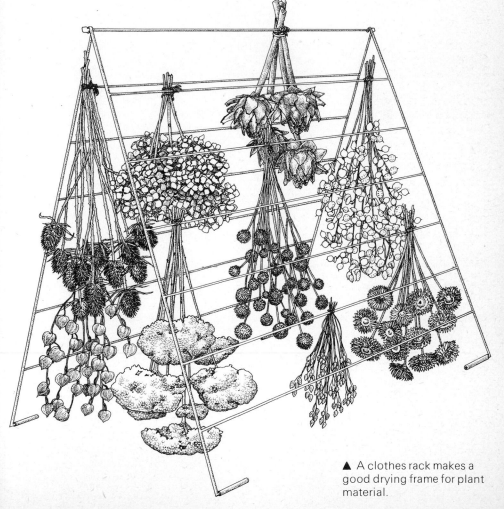

▲ A clothes rack makes a good drying frame for plant material.

▲ Inspiration in designing plaques of dried plant material includes works like this eighteenth-century wood carving by Grinling Gibbons.

▶ A plaque of air-dried and glycerined plant material arranged by Doris Hickson on a board covered with hessian.

borax and sand. There are several books and a good leaflet available giving the method of drying plant material in a desiccant (see p. 92).

Using dried plant material

Strong-stemmed dried plant material can be used in water as long as it is dried in between use. Other dried flowers can be arranged in

all-dried designs and for plaques and pictures.

Dried flowers can be used in normal flower arrangements or in pictures and swags to hang up. A plaque has come to mean, in the language of the flower arranger, a design mounted on a visible background. It may be of any shape, framed or unframed. A swag is similar but the background is invisible.

A plaque

The backing may be made of hardboard, wood or pegboard, cut to any shape. It needs a finish, such as:

1 Wood stain, polished or varnished with matt or shiny lacquer. This is unsuitable for pegboard but attractive on well-sanded wood.

2 Paint such as emulsion, or matt blackboard paint in black or deep green.

3 Cork sheeting, strawcloth,

72

Fablon, reed matting, or wallpaper glued on to the backing and turned over neatly on to the back.

4 Fabric such as linen, felt, thin hessian, textured cotton or jersey. Cut a piece about 2 to 4 cm bigger all round than the backing, to allow it to turn over. Paint over the backing with decorator's size. Allow to dry and give it a second coat. Place on the fabric and rub it for a minute or two with a clean duster. Turn over the edges and mitre the corners, neatly cutting away any surplus fabric. Stick down the turnings, and neaten the edge with sticky tape or brown paper glued over the backing.

Mechanics for plant material

There are several methods:
1 Put a little impact adhesive such as Uhu or Evo-Stik on the back of each piece of plant material and gradually build up the design.
2 Make a mound of slow-drying adhesive such as Clam 2 and insert the plant material.
3 Knock three or four nails into the backing from the front. Cover a dry block of Oasis with plastic netting. Using reel wire, attach the netting to the nails. Arrange the plant material in the foam. This is a temporary device and can be changed or removed.
4 Push any wires on the dried plant material through the holes in pegboard with a fabric covering. Glue on extra plant material to fill in the gaps. This is suitable for

heavy plant material that needs the extra support of wire.

Hanging

Insert two ring screws in the backing and twist on wire or tie on cord for hanging.

A swag

The same basic methods are used to make a swag. The only difference is that the background is not visible and therefore need not be finished with fabric or other covering. It is advisable to paint it in case any part shows through the plant material.

The backing should be a

▲ A plaque by Sarah Marquardt, who drew the design on cardboard, glued on seed pods, cut it out and mounted it on a felt background. The glass was glued to the frame and a 2-cm band of felt-covered cardboard was inserted to hold the glass away from the picture. Long screws attach the backing to the frame.

lot smaller than the intended decoration, so that it cannot be seen, and because the plant material extends from it. Hardboard is usually the most successful as it is light and has holes for securing wired plant material.

PRESSING

Pressed-flower pictures are a permanent decoration that can be made at any time of the year, and are very acceptable as gifts. They use only a few flowers and leaves, available from a garden or from the countryside.

Small flowers and leaves with thin tissue are the most suitable, and should include fine stems and tiny flowers for making new centres for bigger flowers. Thick, many-petalled flowers will not press well, and fleshy plant material is quite unsuitable.

A few flowers such as daffodils can be dissected for pressing in pieces. Pick only perfect specimens on a dry day.

Using a press

Cut off the stems, and place the plant material flat on a piece of blotting paper. Cover with a second piece of blotting paper, rolling it gently over the plant material. Place the flowers in the blotting paper between the pages of a large heavy book—or, preferably, put them in a flower press for results which are tissue thin and very flat. Leave the plant material in the press for at least three months, and preferably for a year, as this improves the colour retention.

During the first ten days the press should be tightened daily as the plant material loses moisture.

It is helpful to press flowers, leaves and stems in separate, labelled sheets. Flower centres can also be pressed separately, to be assembled with loose petals into another flower. Stems can be curved by Sellotaping them into shape.

Colours

Colours can fade during pressing and after exposure to light. Flowers should always be placed in dim lighting. Yellows and oranges keep their colour well. Red and purple may turn brown; but long pressing helps their retention of colour. Pink is successful but blues fade a little; grey and autumn-tinted leaves, have good colour retention, while white can turn beige.

Making a press

A press is not difficult to make. You will need: 2 pieces of thick plywood or chipboard about 25 cm square; 10 sheets of thick cardboard; 18 sheets of blotting paper; and 4 bolts with wing-nuts about 10 cm long.

Drill holes in the corners of the plywood while holding both pieces together so that the top holes are immediately above the lower

▼ A daffodil flower, bisected for pressing.

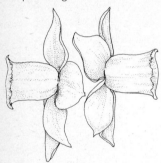

▼ Acanthus petals surrounding a buttercup.

▼ Delphinium petals with barley seeds.

▼ Two passion-flower leaves, reassembled.

▲ In assembling a flower press, place alternate cardboard and blotting-paper layers (**2**) between two boards (**1**). Stems can be curved by fastening with Sellotape (**3**); and labelling (**4**) helps prevent disturbance.

ones, for the bolts to be fitted. Cut the corners off the sheets of cardboard and the blotting paper so that they will lie flat in the press. Starting with a piece of cardboard, add two sheets of blotting paper and then a layer of cardboard alternately, finishing with a sheet of cardboard. Place the whole batch between the pieces of wood, and insert the bolts from the bottom with the wing-nuts on top. The press is now ready for use.

It is advisable not to disturb plant material during pressing and fresh specimens are better added between new sheets of blotting paper on the top. Dating the sheets is helpful.

Storage

Pressed plant material is very lightweight and can easily blow away or become damaged. It is better to store it in the press until it is required for a picture or to transfer in sheets to a box, second press or heavy book.

Making a pressed-flower picture

New or old frames can be used, but normally ones with a light effect are in keeping with pressed flowers, which are delicate in appearance. It is essential for the glass to press against the plant material, and a deep backing is unsuitable. Any shape can be used. Glass is also necessary for protection from dust.

The backing should be rigid, for example hardboard or Daler-board. Thick cardboard and strawboard are also suitable.

Some glues show through the plant material when dry, so experiment with these if you have any doubts. Copydex and Marvin are safe; and Uhu is often used, but only a spot at a time.

The background for the design can be of fabric or paper. In either case a dull surface and a soft colour are advisable, to show off the flowers. Cover the backing completely with decorator's size, using two coats and allowing it to dry in between. Press on the fabric or paper, which should be creaseless.

Make-up

Helpful tools are a small, thin, flat knife, tweezers, cocktail sticks, nail scissors and a fine paintbrush.

The make-up should be done away from draughts, which can easily waft away the plant material. It is helpful to have a board to lay over this if you have to temporarily leave the work.

The design

Try out the design on a sheet of white paper, which will show it up well. The knife is best for lifting the plant material, the tweezers for moving smaller pieces.

Discard any damaged flowers or leaves, remembering that you may be creating an heirloom and will want it to look perfect for many years. Move the design around until you are quite satisfied. The flowers can overlap each other or the leaves or be placed with space between. Stems can be used or not and the design can be naturalistic or more stylized. There are many ideas in books, friezes, paintings, advertisements and illustrations for garlands, posies, flower arrangements, borders and naturalistic groupings. Any shape can be used, and there are no rules.

Transfer the plant material to your prepared backing and, using a cocktail stick, place a spot of glue in one or more places on each piece. Some people have been successful without glue, holding the flowers in place with the glass, but a spot of glue is safer. There is no need to glue the back of each leaf and flower completely—and in fact for reasons of grooming the less used the better.

Clean the glass well and allow it to dry before it is placed on the picture. Methylated spirit is good for this. Try not to move the glass once it is in place because this disturbs the plant ma-

◄ Pressed flowers can be assembled into representational shapes, as in this 'bouquet' by Mrs H. B. King.

▲ A simple pressed-flower picture by the author.

terial. Place the picture in the frame. Another pair of hands can be helpful at this stage.

It may be necessary to pad the backing with paper or card to ensure a tight fit before finally covering with a sheet of brown paper. It is not a good idea to secure the backing with nails, as this could disturb the picture. Masking or brown-paper tape is better for holding the backing in position.

Hanging the picture
Screw eyes can be inserted for hanging up the picture. It is important to place it away from strong light, either natural or artificial. The colours do fade, though pleasingly, in time. It is ex-pected that eventually there will be a solution or powder to help retain the colours of dried plant material.

Greetings cards and calendars
Dried plant material can dec-orate your own cards and be a personal and special gift. Blank cards can be obtained (see p. 91) especially for this, with coverings for pro-tection of the decoration.

Access-ories

Flowers may be combined in an arrangement with man-made objects such as plates, candles, figurines and other ornaments. They also have an easy harmony with many 'found' objects, such as shells and stones, that although not of plant material are created naturally. All such objects are classed by flower arrangers as accessories.

In addition to qualities of their own, accessories are useful for lessening the number of flowers when these are in short supply; for adding interest, even as a 'conversation piece'; and for interpreting themes at a show.

Candles are easy accessories to use, and suitable in arrangements for public and private social events. The simplest use is to stand a chunky candle on top of a round of Oasis, with leaves and then flowers added around the base. If you prefer flowers lifted up, place Oasis in a candlecup on a candlestick, and make a hole, using a knife, in its centre to take a narrow candle, or use a specially made metal candle-

holder. Add flowers and leaves as before. An alternative method is to omit the candlecup and place a candle securely in a candlestick. Make a hole through a round of Oasis and push it on to the candle until it is about halfway down. Allow it to drip water for a while after adding the flowers. They will not last long, but will make a quick decoration for a special event.

Brightly coloured candles tend to vie with the flowers. Creams, greens, browns and soft colours are a better buy. Plant material, especially if it is dried, should be kept well away from candle flames.

Shells with varying textures and shapes can be placed at the side of flowers. It is easier to group them on

a base before arranging the flowers. Shells are especially suitable in hot temperatures, as they give a sense of coolness. They can also be used to interpret a sea-shore. In doing this, use the correct shells for the country.

Plates, paintings, ornaments and figurines, when used in arrangements, should be positioned before the plant material so that they become incorporated into the design and do not look like an afterthought. A base is useful for uniting the accessory and the flowers. The colours of an accessory can be repeated in the plant material; this also gives a sense of unity.

At home there can be complete freedom; but in a competitive show judges feel that plant material should predominate over accessories.

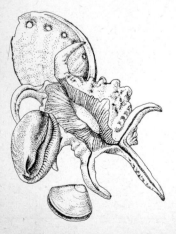

Flower shows

Once the basic skills of flower arranging have been mastered, it is always an exciting and interesting challenge to enter a local flower show. This provides a good opportunity to meet other flower arrangers and to learn from them. It is also the way most of the better flower arrangers have improved their skills.

Your local flower arrangement show may be put on by a flower arrangement club; or it may be part of a horticultural show. Some classes in flower arranging are limited to flower club members and others are open to anyone. But all the details are given in the show schedule, which should be read very carefully. It is obtainable from the show secretary, whose address can be found from the local press, council, library or from knowledgeable individuals.

Each exhibitor is allocated space for an exhibit, and details of size and shape are given. It is sensible to have a 'mock-up' a week or two in advance to try out your arrangement for size and shape and for its contents. It is also helpful to know what qualities the judges look for. They will be:

1 Conformity to the show schedule—for example if it says a space of 30 cm is allowed for the exhibit you will be eliminated if you have taken up 45 cm.
2 Condition of plant material: wilted plant material is not often awarded a prize.
3 The design, to be judged in terms of the way you have

assembled your plant material—to see for example if you have included emphasis flowers, leaves or fruit.
4 Staging and grooming: this covers the presentation of exhibits, which should be clean, tidy and suitably proportioned to their niches.
5 Distinction, a criterion that covers any special qualities your arrangement may have, such as unusual plant material or a clever accessory.
6 Schedule interpretation, which is essential. You may have followed the schedule to the letter but you must also make sure that the class

title is interpreted. If for example the title is 'Country Lane' then an oriental base will not be suitable, nor expensive plant material.

Interpretation
Much of the fun of shows lies in searching for suitable accessories with which to interpret a theme. An enormous variety can readily be acquired or borrowed; but they should not dominate the flowers and should be in keeping with them. Above all it is useful and interesting to see how other arrangers have interpreted the same title.

▶ 'Romance and the Rose' by Mrs D. Iddon, at an annual show.

Useful plants to grow

In planning to grow shrubs for use as material in flower arrangements it is important to remember that they must be allowed to grow for a few years before they can be cut without damage. Foliage plants are a necessity because it is usually easier to buy flowers than foliage.

After a basic collection has been planted, other plants can be added as you find varieties that you like, bearing in mind the size of your garden and the climate and soil conditions. Normally plants that grow well in local nurseries, garden centres and gardens of stately houses can be assumed to enjoy similar conditions to those in your own garden and are more reliable than plants ordered from nurseries with a different climate. All the plants listed below are likely to prove useful.

Shrubs

Aucuba japonica longifolia (laurel)
Plain leaves for concealing mechanics (see p. 50).
Berberis thunbergii atropurpurea (barberry)
Small, maroon leaves in long sprays.
Buxus sempervirens latifolia maculata (box)
Small, long-lasting, green leaves.
Camellia japonica
Glossy, green leaves that last well; pretty flowers.
Chamaecyparis obtusa crippsii (cypress)
Golden foliage in fern-like sprays.
Choisya ternata (Mexican orange blossom)
Useful rosette-shaped leaves.
Corylus avellana contorta (corkscrew hazel)
Very curved branches, for winter use; quick-growing.
Cotoneaster cornubia
Red berries for use in autumn (see p. 13).
Cytisus praecox (broom)
Slender, curved stems; cream flowers in spring.
Elaeagnus: 'Limelight'; or *E.pungens variegata*; or *E.macrophylla*
Attractive, evergreen leaves splashed yellow.
Escallonia: 'Apple Blossom'
Pink flowers in long sprays, in summer; evergreen foliage.
Euonymus fortunei: 'Silver Queen'
Green leaves with cream edges.
Fatsia japonica (aralia)
Large, lobed, green leaves, good for big designs.
Garrya elliptica
Green-grey catkins, in late winter.
Hydrangea: 'Hortensia'
Varieties in several colours of flowers; useful for drying.
Hypericum calycinum (Rose of Sharon)
Black fruits in autumn.
Ilex aquifolium: 'Bacciflava'
A yellow-berried holly (see p. 13).
Ilex aquifolium: 'Golden Queen'
Holly with gold and green leaves.
Ligustrum ovalifolium aureum (golden privet)
Straight sprays of leaves, light green-gold.
Mahonia: 'Charity'
Long, spiny leaflets; evergreen; preserves well.
Pittosporum crassifolium
Good, rosette-shaped leaves.
Pyracantha atalantioides
Red berries, in autumn and winter.
Rosa rubrifolia
Blue-grey foliage.
Ruta graveolens (rue)
Small, blue-green leaves (see p. 12).
Salix setsuka
Fasciated branches useful in modern styles of arrangement.
Skimmia foremanii
Red berries, in autumn.
Spiraea bumalda: 'Gold Flame'
Hybrid with good-coloured foliage; small leaves, in sprays.
Symphoricarpos albus laevigatus (snowberry)
White berries, in winter.
Thuya plicata aureovariegata
Yellow and green, fern-like foliage.
Viburnum opulus
Red fruits, in autumn.
Vinca major elegantissima (periwinkle)
Trailing foliage (see p. 12).
Weigela florida variegata
Flowering branches in summer; cream-edged leaves.

Perennials

Achillea (yarrow): 'Coronation gold'
Deep yellow flowers; useful for drying.
Alchemilla mollis (lady's mantle)
Small, bright, yellow-green flowers, useful round leaves, in summer.
Anaphalis margaritacea (pearly everlasting)
Small white flowers, in summer; useful for drying.
Arum italicum pictum
Useful winter foliage.
Astilbe (false goat's head)
Plume-like heads of pink, white and red flowers, in summer.
Astrantia major (Hattie's pincushion)
Small, pink and white flowers in summer; good for pressing.
Bergenia cordifolia
Large, round, evergreen leaves, all year; invaluable for concealing mechanics.
Briza maxima (quaking grass)
Suitable for drying.
Bromus (ornamental oats)
Suitable for drying.

Cineraria maritima: 'Diamond'
Grey leaves.
Cortaderia (pampas grass)
Tall, plumed grass.
Cynara cardunculus (cardoon)
Round or conical heads, in
autumn; serrated leaves.
Cynara scolymus (globe
artichoke)
Similar to above, but larger.
Delphinium
Useful flowers for drying.
Delphinium consolida
(larkspur)
Flowers for drying. (See pp. 50,
74.)
Digitalis (foxglove)
Good seedheads for preserving.
Dipsacus fullonum (teasel)
Good seedheads for drying.
Echinops ritro (globe thistle)
Blue, rounded flowers, useful for
drying.
*Eryngium alpinum, E. giganteum,
E. variifolium* (sea hollies)
Good for drying and preserving.
Helichrysum bracteatum
(straw flower)
Easy to dry (see p. 13).
Helipterum roseum (everlasting)
Small daisy-like flowers for
drying.
Hosta
Many varieties; all are useful for
their plain or variegated leaves,
both large and small (see p. 50).
Lagurus ovatus (hare's tail grass)
Good for drying (see p. 13).
Limonium sinuatum (statice)
Small flowers for drying.
Lunaria annua (honesty)
Silver seedheads and good,
plain leaves (see p. 13).
Macleaya cordata (plume
poppy)
Tall stems of small brown
flowers, in summer.
Onopordum acanthium
(Scotch thistle)
Big, grey leaves.
Paeonia (peony)
Flowers generally red,
sometimes pink or white.
Papaver orientale (oriental
poppy)
Useful flowers, in summer; also

seedheads (see p. 13).
Phormium tenax (New Zealand
flax)
Sword-like leaves; evergreen
(see p. 12).
Physalis franchetii (Chinese
lantern)
Orange seedheads.
Phytolacca americana
(American pokeberry)
Black fruit in autumn; not
edible.
Sedum spectabile (ice-plant)
Useful flowers and leaves.

Annuals
Amaranthus caudatus
(love-lies-bleeding)
Trailing green or red flowers.
Angelica archangelica
A tall biennial with green
flowers and seedheads.
Nicandra physaloides (shoo-fly
plant)
For seedheads.
Nigella damascena (love-in-a-
mist)
Small seedheads.
Papaver somniferum
For seedheads and good
flowers.
Pelargonium (geranium)
For leaves. Not an annual, but
cuttings should be taken each
year (see p. 12).
Verbascum bombyciferum
(mullein)
Good leaves
Triticum (ornamental wheat)
For drying.

Bulbs
Most spring flowering bulbs are
useful for flower arrangement.
*Allium afflatuense, A.
giganteum, A. porrum* (leek)
Rounded flower heads which
dry.
Crocosmia masonorum
Seedheads for drying.
Curtonus paniculatus
Long slender leaves.
Iris foetidissima
Orange seeds.
I. pallida dalmatica
Tall, narrow leaves (see p. 50).

Gladiolus
For flowers and long leaves.

Climbers
Hedera (ivy)
Any variety, for trails (see p. 50).
*Lonicera japonica
aureoreticulata*
(Japanese honeysuckle)

To avoid disappointment it is
sensible to try to see plants at a
local nursery or garden before
buying, or to look them up in a
catalogue or plant book.
Also take the advice of your
nursery man about their
suitability for your garden.

A flower arranger's collection

A stock of plants and equipment
for flower arranging can be
gradually built up and proves
invaluable, both for arranging
flowers at home or elsewhere.
It is part of the interest of flower
arranging to search for
containers, plants, accessories,
equipment and information.

SOURCES
Countryside
Although most wild flowers
should not be picked because of
the need for conservation, there
are many natural objects that
can be collected in the country
and that are plentiful. Anything
on private land should not be
removed without permission;
and restraint is important at all
times. The following items may
each be useful at some time:
driftwood and branches;
ferns for pressing and for fresh
    arrangements;
berries for autumn arrangements;
lichen and fungi;

bulrushes and grasses;
moss for covering mechanics;
stones in many colours;
bark, and small chunks of wood,
    for concealing mechanics;
willow and hazel catkins;
pine cones of many varieties;
foliage for fresh arrangements
    and for preserving;
small wild flowers, and leaves,
    for pressing;
seedheads, especially in autumn;
ivy trails, stems and leaves;
skeletonized leaves and
    seedheads;
disused birds'-nests for
    including in an arrangement
    in the Flemish flower-
    painting style;
feathers

Seashore
shells and coral;
grasses;
stones and pebbles;
driftwood;
weathered flotsam and jetsam;
seaweed to press;
fishermen's floats;
old fishing net;
sand, for mechanics and for use
    in drying flowers

Museums, art galleries, stately homes and art shops
postcards and prints of flower
    arrangements;
Christmas cards of flower
    arrangements;
notes of the surroundings in
    stately houses for period
    arrangements;
postcards and notes of paintings
    using colour schemes that
    interest you, to repeat in an
    arrangement;
museum reproductions of vases
    and potential accessories

Cities and towns
Fabric remnants and short
    lengths, for making bases;
containers, bases and
    accessories of many types
    from markets, shops,
    potteries, antique centres, or
craft studios;
candles in suitable colours;
marble and stone from
    stonemasons;
flowers and equipment from
    florists;
oddments from 'Do it yourself'
    shops, ironmongers, and
    hardware stores—such as
    wire netting, dowel sticks,
    wood, tiles for bases, and
    drainpipes—to adapt into
    containers, bowls, dishes;
flower arrangement and
    gardening books in libraries
    and bookshops;
exhibitions of works of art for
    ideas;
shop windows for ideas in
    decorations;
hotels and restaurants for
    styles of flower arrangement;
theatre production sets for
    colour schemes and design;
design centres for observing
    good design

KEEPING A NOTEBOOK
A notebook is a great asset in
collecting information on flower
arranging. If you attend any
sort of class you will be required
to keep one. It should be
loose-leaf, and contain dividers
to make reference easy. It can be
separated into:
1 Plants to collect.
2 Pictures of flower
arrangements, including
sketches made at shows and
demonstrations.
3 Lists of plants and objects
seen, in a variety of scenes.
4 Recipes and methods for
arranging flowers.
5 Articles about flower
arrangement.
6 Articles about gardening and
plants.

Sources
1 Newspapers and magazines
often have pictures and articles
that are useful to clip out for
insertion in a notebook on
flower arranging.
2 Drawings can be made at
shows and demonstrations.
Even if you cannot draw
artistically, labelled diagrams
can be useful for future
information.
3 Containers seen at museums
and art galleries can be sketched.
4 Photographs can be taken
whenever permitted of flower
arrangements at shows and
demonstrations.
5 A record of your own
arrangements can be made,
using inexpensive camera
equipment, or by means of
drawings.
6 A walk in a garden centre and
the grounds of a stately home at
different seasons of the year is
invaluable for observing plants
that you find attractive. Their
names should be written down
so that they can be ordered in
the future.
7 Demonstrators and lecturers
at flower clubs often give the
names of plants for flower
arrangement that can usefully be
added to your list.
8 Show schedules make
interesting reading for reference
and are worth collecting.
9 Names of books should be
noted that you have seen or that
you hear referred to by a
demonstrator or teacher.

Flowers from florists

Florist's flowers are normally
long-lasting because they are
varieties grown specifically for
the cut-flower trade. They also
travel well.
    No conditioning is necessary
except re-cutting of the stem
ends before arranging the
flowers. This is because the

stems will have been without water during the journey home and a seal may have begun to form over the end.

Most florists sell flowers at the peak of freshness, and well-conditioned. There are, however, some buys better than others, and signs that indicate age:

Centres
Young flowers normally have light yellow centres, and those of older ones are darker. Loose pollen is a sign of age.

Foliage
Leaves should appear fresh and not limp. Dry and brown leaves can be an indication of old age. Leaves which are wilting can be revived, but it is preferable to buy flowers in good condition to save time at home.

Stems
These should be green and not floppy (unless you want them this way). Slimy and brown-marked stems should be avoided.

Petals
Falling petals are a sign of age. Chrysanthemums should have tightly curled petals at the centre, unless they are single. Those with loose petals at the centre should be avoided; but drooping outer petals are of no concern. Crepey petals are a sign of old age, although with some flowers such as freesias and lilies older flowers may be removed and young flowers will remain on the stem.

Whole flowers
Whenever possible buy in bud, especially in the case of spring flowers. The life of the flower is longer in your home if you start with buds. Carnations can be in bud or more open, but should be avoided when a white 'strand' shows in the centre.

LILIES
(In trade terms for their names.)
Arum: 'Richard II'; early spring to late autumn; white and yellow
Auratum: 'The Golden Rayed Lily'; summer; white flowers with yellow band down petal, spotted crimson; large
Candidum: 'Madonna lily'; summer and autumn; short trumpet, white
Eucheris; summer and autumn; pure white
Hansonii; summer; golden yellow, maroon spots
'Henry II'; autumn; orange-yellow
Longiflorum: 'Harrisii'; spring to autumn
Martagon; summer; reflexed flowers, light purple, spotted black
Regale album; summer; white
Rubrum; summer; white, flushed purple on back
Speciosum album; summer and autumn; reflex white flowers
Speciosum melpomene; summer and autumn; white, spotted crimson
Speciosum roseum; summer and autumn; white, spotted pink
Speciosum rubrum; summer and autumn; white, spotted carmine
Tenuifolium; summer; scarlet Turk's-cup flowers
Tigrinum splendens: 'Tiger Lily'; autumn; fiery orange, spotted crimson
Umbellatum: 'Golden Fleece', 'Orange Triumph'; orange-yellow, purple spots. 'Splendidum'; vermilion, shaded crimson. 'Vermilion Brilliant'.
All flower during summer.

ROSES
Pink
Briarcliffe
Bridal Wreath
Carine
Carole
Cerise Garnette
Chiffon
Edith Helen
Floriade
Gigi
Hollywood
Junior Miss
Lady Sylvia
Madam Butterfly
Nymph
Pink Frills
Pink Sensation
Rose Garnette
Salmon Pink G.
Sweet Seventeen

Red
Baccara
Better Times
Forever Yours
Garnette
Happiness
Lovita
Mary Hart
New Yorker
Nordia
Pearl of Aalsmeer
Poinsettia

Blue and mauve
Blue Moon
Sterling Silver

White
Clarice Goodacre
Iceberg
Tiara
Virgo

Yellow
Dr Verhauge
Duisberg
Golden Garnette
Guisby
Roselandia
Spanish Sun
Tawny Gold

Apricot and orange
Autumn
Belinda
Circus
Henrietta Pechtold
Interflora
Jingles
Katherine Pechtold

Madam Offman
Peach Orange Garnette
Promis
Queen
Rumba
Sunset Garnette
Superstar
Talisman
Veleta
Zorina

TULIPS
Red and variations
Allbright
Aureole
Bartigon
Bonanza
Campfire
Crater
Dover
Dubonnet
Edith Eddy
Elmus
Farncombe Saunders
Galway
Hadley
Hollands Glory
Korneforus
Krelages Triumph
Lefeber's Favourite
Merry Widow
Olgar
Parade
Paris
Paul Richter
Princess Beatrix
Red Matador
Red Pitt
Rhineland
Roland
Scarlet O'Hara
Scarlet Sensation
Spring Song
Top Score
Trophy
Von der Berden
William Pitt

Orange
Afterglow
Apeldoorn
Apricot Beauty
Bruno Walter
Dillenburg
General De Wet
John Gay

London
Orange Triumph
Orange Wonder
Oxford
William of Orange

Yellow
Belona
Christmas Gold
December Gold
Golden Age
Golden Harvest
Hoangho
Inglescombe Yellow
Judoshnik
Mamasa
Niphetos
Ornament
Reforma
Rijnsoever
Sulphur
Sulphur Cloud
Sulphur Triumph
Sunkist
Sweet Harmony
Yellow Gem
Yellow Giant

Pink
Aristocrat
Clara Butt
Queen Augusta
Queen of Bartigens
Peach Blossom
Peerless Pink
Philip Snowden
Pink Attraction
Pink Glow
Pride of Haarlem
Pride of Zwananburg
Princess Elizabeth
Prunus
Rose Copeland
The Peach

Mauve and purple
Algiba
Blue Amiable
Copeland's Rival
Dreaming Maid
First Lady
George Grappe
Insurpassable
Orient Express
Pandion
Piquant

Queen of the Night
Scotch Lassie
The Bishop
Wm Copeland

CHRYSANTHEMUM BLOOMS
Yellow
Alec Bedser
Bagshot Yellow
Balcombe Yellow
Beacon
Charles Rowe
Delightful
Golden Rule
Golden Sweetheart
Hansmoor Glory
Harlequin
Imperial Yellow
J. R. Johnson
Marie Brunton
Marlene
Medea
Moonbeam
Primrose Cricket
Spinning Gold
Sun Avon
Yellow Fred Shoesmith
Yellow Marvel
Yellow Snowdance

White
American Beauty
Bessie Rowe
Ermine
Evelyn Bush
Favourite
Fred Shoesmith
Madonna
Pennine Snow
Rivalry
White Hope Valley
White John Woolman
White Loveliness

Bronze and red
Alert
Balcombe Perfection
Birmingham
Brenda
Bronze Brietner
Carefree
Chatsworth
Christmas Red
Christmas Wine
Copper Utopia

Covent Garden
Denard
Escort
Florence Shoesmith
Gloucester
Hurricane
Inferno
Mayfield Crimson
Nicholas Zwater
Packwell
Parade
Pennant
Peter Shoesmith
Radar
Red Balcombe Perfection
Red Flare
Tom Pierce
Typhoon
Westfield Bronze
Woking Perfection

Mauve, maroon and wine
Florence Harwood
Mauve Princess
Moorlands Purple
Moorlands Wine
Wyvern Maroon

Pink
Amy Shoesmith
Brenda Talbot
Brian Clark
Brietner
Catherine Porter
Cessbury
Day Dream
Hazel Swager
Imperial Pink
Julie Ann
Loveliness
Margaret Swager
Milestone
New Princess
Pinksmoor
Rose Brietner
Rose Sylvia Riley
Salmon Sweetheart
Silver Rose
Sweetheart
Sylvia Riley
Una

Peach and apricot
Aileen
Apricot Brenda Talbot
Apricot Princess Ann

SPRAY CHRYSANTHEMUMS

Yellow
Buckskin	Pale single; buff yellow
Golden Elegance	Single; short petal
Hayday	Deep yellow double
Imperial	Soft yellow; large flower
Lemon Polaris	Single; short petal
Yellow Bonnie Jean	Single; short petal
Yellow Elegance	Soft yellow; loose petals; double
Yellow Galaxy	Single; long petals; deep yellow
Yellow Icecap	Single; long petals; deep yellow
Yellow Shasta	Long ray petals; anemone centre
Yellow Taffeta	Single; long petals; deep yellow

Pink and mauve-pink
Almega	Pink
Alveda	Large mauve double
Blue Chip	Mauve-pink
Cherry Chip	Mauve-pink
Delamere	Single mauve-pink
Delight	Wine colour
Delmarvel	Mauve-pink; large flower
Excello	Mauve-pink; pale centre; double
Portrait	Pink; round reflex petals

Red and bronze-apricot
Apricot Sybil	Apricot; pinkish sheen
Cardinal	Red; small flowers; open sprays
Dragon	Double; deep bronze
Galaxy	Pale bronze; single
Inferno	Red; very tight eye
Jet Fire	Red-bronze
Mermaid	Bronze
Orange Bougarde	Orange reflex
Red Delight	Red-bronze
Red Matador	Bronze; anemone eye
Red Medalion	Bronze; anemone eye
Rubyatt	Red-bronze
Sybil	Pale bronze; long petals; single
Tangiers	Bronze; anemone centre
Thelma	Dusty red; single
Tuneful	Orange-bronze; single

CARNATIONS

Allwood's Crimson	Crimson
Alsmeers Glory	Very dark red
Anne	Tangerine pink
Apricot Sim	Apricot pink
Arthur Sim	White ground; red tips
Asa Thor	Yellow, striped red
Ashington Pink	Pale shell pink
Astrid	Striped pink
Bailey's Apricot	Apricot
Ballerina	Deep cerise pink
Bidini	Yellow

Apricot Sylvia Riley
Bill Riley
Carefree
Egerton Sweetheart
Fred Yule
Peach Blossom

White

Bonnie Jean
Cloudbank
Cloudburst
Coronardo
Dawn Star
Elegance
Ermine
Hurricane
Iceberg
Icecap
Long Island
Momento
Polaris
Shasta
Snow Crest
White Tops

CARNATIONS

Blue Sydney	Blue-pink
Brigadoon	Clear yellow
Brighton Rock	Salmon, boldly marked with scarlet
Brocade	White, heavily overlaid with crimson
Calypso Sim	Bright shocking pink
Canadian Pink	Bright rose pink
Caravelle Red	Bright red
Cardinal	Bright orange-red
Clove	Crimson
Cocome Sim	Variegated: apricot orange, marked red
Coquet	Pale pink
Coral Glow	Coral pink
Crimson Sim	Crimson
Crowley Sim	Light pink
Dainty Lady	Sulphur yellow ground; edged with rose-scarlet
Dark Red Sim	Crimson
Dazzler	Bright red; yellow markings at base
Deep Pink Sim	Deep shell pink
Delight	Deep mauve-pink magenta
Desire	Similar, but paler than Pink Diamond (see below)
Dusty Sim	Dusky rose pink
Edna Samuel	Deep salmon pink
Elizabeth	Tangerine pink
Fanfare	Deep lilac
Favourite	Medium pink
Flamingo Sim	Flamingo pink
Florida	Dirty cream
Fragrant Ann	Large white
Frosty Sim	Cerise with white tips
Golden Gleam	Rich yellow; marked with scarlet
Golden Rain	Clear pale gold
Green Ice	Greenish white
Harvest Moon	Apricot yellow
Heather Beauty	Mauve-pink
Helios	Clear primrose yellow
Hick's Triumph	Crimson
Hollywood Sim	Scarlet, flushed pink at tips
Hunting Pink	Salmon scarlet
Ice Cap	Pure white
Janice	Orchid pink
Joker	Deep crimson
Laddie Sim	Salmon pink
Lady Eve Price	Cerise, barred maroon
Lavender Lady	Orchid mauve
Lemon Sim	Lemon yellow
Lochinvar Louise	Deep magenta, shaded to pale

Lolita	Deep shocking pink
Manderine Sim	Deep tangerine red
Marchioness	Deep pink
Margaret	Rich claret
Margaret Kay	White
Marie Antoinette	Delicate pink
Mary	Deep salmon pink
Mary Aylsworth	Petunia rose
Midas	Clear yellow
Monty's Apricot	Apricot yellow
Monty's Pale Rose	Pale rose pink
Northland	White
Old Rose	Deep rose
Ondine	Deep pink
Orchid Sim	Mauve; pale edges
Pagee	Yellow
Paris	Light salmon pink
Peppermint	Similar to Arthur Sim
Peterson's Pink	Pale pink; deeper than Pink Sim (see below)
Phares	Mauve-pink
Pike's Peak	Similar to Frosty Sim
Pink Diamond	White, heavily marked with red
Pink Sim	Pale shell pink
Portrait	Deep rose pink
Princess Anne	Deep shell pink
Red Majestic	Bright scarlet
Robert Allwood	Vivid scarlet
Rovi	Deep coral pink
Royalette	Deep lavender pink
Royalty	Lavender pink
Safari	Deep cerise pink
Sagus	White
Sally Jones	Deep salmon pink
Saskia	White
Scania	Scarlet
Seley	Pale salmon pink
Serenade	Mauve, striped cerise
Shot Silk	Old rose with bold scarlet stripes
Skyline	Chrome-apricot ground, flecked scarlet
Snow Maiden	Pure white
Tangerine Sim	Tangerine
Topsy	Deep red
White Sim	White, sometimes flecked red
William Sim	Bright red
Wivelsfield's Crimson	Crimson
Zunessa	Heliotrope, striped purple, red and cerise
Zuni	Dark cerise, flecked crimson-maroon

Classes and opportunities

Classes and opportunites

Classes in flower arranging are held by flower arranging and garden clubs throughout the world. In the United Kingdom they are also held in local adult education centres and colleges of further education. Information about days, times and types of courses available can be obtained from your local college, library or Council Education Officer. Lists of courses available are published in local newspapers in the early autumn.

Courses vary both in content and in length, from six weeks onwards. In addition to flower arranging, there are courses on related subjects including horticulture, botany and design. Specific subjects are also covered, such as making Christmas decorations; drying and preserving flowers; arranging church flowers; doing period flower arrangements, and specifically economical arrangements; and making plaques and swags.

Certificates can be obtained in flower arranging which have a national standard. The City and Guilds of London Institute offers examinations following courses in colleges of adult education: the Part One course, for beginners and intermediate standard students, lasts 300 hours; Part Two, for advanced students and those who have passed the Part One course, lasts 200 hours. For each part there is a candidate fee of £4.25; and there are three component fees for Part One of £1.10 each, and two for Part Two of £2.70. Usually classes meet once a week, in the daytime or in the evening.

Learning further skills

Once you have learnt to arrange flowers and are reasonably proficient, thought can be given to going further than doing arrangements only in your own home. You can undertake the following:

1 Compete in local, area and international shows.
2 Exhibit, through your flower arranging club in the festivals and exhibitions organized in stately houses and buildings such as museums and art galleries.
3 Become a freelance flower arranger in hotels, offices and restaurants, and for private parties.
4 Volunteer to arrange flowers in a hospital or old people's home, by writing to the matron or administrator.
5 Join a local church flower guild.
6 Train through your club to become a demonstrator and/or judge of flower arranging.
7 Take further courses in floristry, and become a florist.
8 Participate in the administration of a flower club and volunteer to undertake typing, accounting, show organization, catering or help to run a sales table or library.
9 Train to be a teacher of flower arranging. Normally this can be done after passing the City and Guilds of London Institute examinations, Parts One and Two.

Suppliers and nurseries

Bulbs

Broadleigh Gardens,
Barr House,
Bishops Hull,
Taunton,
Somerset
Telephone: 0823 86231

Jefferson-Brown,
Lakeside,
Whitbourne,
Worcestershire
Telephone: 088 62 270
For daffodils.

Orpington Nurseries,
Rocky Lane,
Gatton Park,
Merstham,
Surrey
Telephone: 649 2221

Van Tubergen Ltd,
Willow Bank Wharf,
Ranelagh Gardens,
London, SW6
Telephone: 01 736 2313

Wallace and Barr Ltd,
The Nurseries,
Marden,
Kent
Telephone: 0622 831235

Walter Blom and Son Ltd,
Coombelands Nurseries,
Leavesden,
Watford,
Hertfordshire
Telephone: 092 73 72071

Dahlias

Aylett Nurseries Ltd,
North Orbital Road,

London Colney,
St Albans,
Hertfordshire
Telephone: 61 22255

Ferns
Fibrex Nurseries Ltd,
Harvey Road,
Evesham,
Worcestershire
Telephone: 0386 6190

Reginald Kaye Ltd,
Waithman Nurseries,
Silverdale,
Carnforth,
Lancashire
Telephone: 0524 701252

Houseplants
Rochfords,
Turnford Hall Nurseries,
Turnford
Broxbourne,
Hertfordshire;
and:
Forest Road,
Cotebrook,
Tarporley,
Cheshire
Telephone: 61 64512 and
082921 395/485

Perennials
Beth Chatto,
White Barn House,
Elmstead Market,
Colchester,
Essex
Telephone: 020 622 2007
For unusual plants.

Blackmore and Langdon Ltd,
Pensford Nursery,
Bristol
Telephone: 027 589 2300
For delphiniums.

Bressingham Gardens,
Bressingham,
Diss,
Norfolk
Telephone: 037 988 464

Bees Ltd,
Sealand,

Chester,
Cheshire
Telephone: 024 458 501

Great Dixter Nurseries,
Northiam,
East Sussex
Telephone: 079 3160

Hayes,
Ambleside,
Cumbria
Telephone: 096 63 3434

John Scott and Co.,
The Royal Nurseries,
Merriott,
Somerset
Telephone: 0460 72306

Kelways Nurseries,
Langport,
Somerset
Telephone: 0458 250521
For irises and peonies.

Margery Fish Nursery,
East Lambrook Manor,
South Petherton,
Somerset
Telephone: 0460 40328

R. Poland,
Brook House Nursery,
Highbrook Road,
Ardingly,
West Sussex
Telephone: 0444 892555

Treasures of Tenbury Ltd,
Tenbury Wells,
Worcestershire
Telephone: 0584 810777

Treseders' Nurseries (Truro) Ltd,
Moresk Road,
Truro,
Cornwall
Telephone: 0872 4371

Underwood's,
Baker's Lane,
Colchester,
Essex
Telephone: 0206 72050
For grey foliage.

Roses
James Cocker and Sons,
Whitmyres,
Lang Stracht,
Aberdeen
Telephone: 0224 33261

Fryers Nurseries Ltd,
Knutsford,
Cheshire
Telephone: 0565 2642

C. Gregory and Son Ltd,
The Rose Garden,
Toton Lane,
Stapleford,
Nottinghamshire
Telephone: 0602 395454

Harkness and Co. Ltd,
The Rose Gardens,
Hitchin,
Hertfordshire
Telephone: 0462 4027

E. B. LeGrice (Roses) Ltd,
Roseland Nurseries,
North Walsham,
Norfolk
For varieties of roses with
unusual colours.

John Mattock Ltd,
Nuneham Courtenay,
Oxfordshire
Telephone: 086 738 265

Meilland Star Roses Ltd,
464 Goffs Lane,
Goffs Oak,
Waltham Cross,
Hertfordshire

Sunningdale Nurseries Ltd,
The Waterer Group,
Windlesham,
Surrey
Telephone: 0990 20496
Also for useful varieties of trees
and shrubs.

Wheatcroft Roses Ltd,
Landmere Lane,
Edwalton,
Nottingham
Telephone: 0602 216061

Seeds

Dickson, Brown and Tait Ltd,
Timperley,
Altrincham,
Cheshire
Telephone: 061 973 2214
This firm also supplies bulbs.

Samuel Dobie and Sons Ltd,
Upper Dee Mills,
Llangollen,
Clwyd

Sutton and Sons Ltd,
Torquay,
Devon
Telephone: 0803 62011

Thompson and Morgan Ltd,
London Road,
Ipswich,
Suffolk
Telephone: 0473 214226

Unwin Ltd,
Histon,
Cambridgeshire
Telephone: 022 023 2270

Trees and Shrubs

Bodnant Gardens Nursery,
Colwyn Bay,
Clwyd
Telephone: 049 267 460

Hillier and Sons,
Winchester,
Hampshire
Telephone: 0962 69245

Notcutt's Nurseries Ltd,
Woodbridge,
Suffolk
Telephone: 039 43 3344

Reuthe Ltd,
Foxhill Nurseries,
Jackass Lane,
Keston,
Kent
Telephone: 66 52249

R.V. Roger Ltd,
The Nurseries,
Pickering,
North Yorkshire
Telephone: 0751 72226

Roseacre Garden Centre,
Kidderminster Road South,
West Hagley,
Worcestershire
Telephone: 0562 700552

Russell Ltd,
Richmond Nurseries,
Windlesham,
Surrey
Telephone: 0990 21411

South Down Nurseries,
Redruth,
Cornwall
Telephone: 0209 216194

Toynbee Ltd,
Yapton Road,
Barnham,
West Sussex
Telephone: 0243 552121

The above nurseries may sell additional plants to those shown, in which they are specialists. There are many local nurseries which supply plants of all varieties. It is sensible to try local nurseries and garden centres in the first instance to save postage and also because the plants have probably been grown in similar climatic conditions to those in your own garden.

Plants should be ordered by their botanical name and not the vernacular name (sometimes called common or popular name), which changes between different countries and localities.

Cut flowers can be bought from local florists, nurseries and markets. Markets, for the sale of flowers wholesale, also supply individuals other than florists but the flowers must be bought in larger quantities than in a florist's shop.

Cut flowers by post

K.B.M. Shirley and Co. Ltd,
306 Flower Market,
New Covent Garden,
London, SW8
Telephone: 01 720 7129
Minimum order £10.

Notton,
Lacock,
Chippenham,
Wiltshire
Also dried flowers. List
available.

Other suppliers

See *The Flower Arranger* and *Flora* magazines for up-to-date addresses of suppliers of dried flowers, blank greetings cards, driftwood, containers, accessories, mechanics, fabrics, tools, ironwork, frames, adhesives and desiccants.

Slides and films

Slides of flower arrangements can be hired from:
The National Association of Flower Arrangement Societies of Great Britain,
21a Denbigh Street,
London SW1
Telephone: 01 828 5145
Films on flower arrangement can be hired from:
Gerard Holdsworth Productions Ltd,
31 Palace Street,
London SW1
Telephone: 01 828 1671

Organizations

The National Association of Flower Arrangement Societies of Great Britain (NAFAS),
21a Denbigh Street,
London SW1
Telephone: 01 828 5145
For addresses of flower arranging clubs throughout the United Kingdom, including Northern Ireland, and the Republic of Ireland; and information on any aspect of flower arranging.

The National Council of State Garden Clubs Inc., USA,
4401 Magnolia Avenue,
St Louis,
Missouri 63110, USA
For addresses of American clubs.

The Royal Horticultural Society,
Vincent Square,
London SW1
Telephone: 01 834 4333
Membership includes a monthly magazine among other benefits.

Ikebana International,
CPO. Box 1262,
Tokyo, Japan

The City and Guilds of London Institute,
46 Britannia Street,
London WC1
Telephone: 01 278 2468
For all information regarding flower arrangement examinations.

The Royal National Rose Society,
Bone Hill,
Chiswell Green Lane,
St Albans,
Hertfordshire
Telephone: 56 50461
For details of membership, and an annual publication.

Interflora Headquarters,
Interflora House,
Sleaford,
Lincolnshire
Telephone: 0529 304141

The National Gardens Scheme,
57 Lower Belgrave Square,
London SW1
Telephone: 01 730 0355

The National Trust,
42 Queen Anne's Gate,
London SW1
Telephone: 01 930 0211

Books, leaflets and magazines

BOOKS ON FLOWER ARRANGEMENT
A History of Flower Arrangement, Julia Berrall, Thames and Hudson. Many illustrations of period flower arrangements.

European Flower Painters, Peter Mitchell, C. & A. Black, 1973, £7.50. Inspirational book for period and traditional designs.

Design for Flower Arrangers, Dorothy Reister, Van Nostrand 1972, £3.50. Advanced design for flower arrangers.

Creative Flower Arrangement, Jean Taylor, Stanley Paul, 1973, £3.75 and £2.50. A comprehensive book for students.

Flowers in Church, Jean Taylor, Mowbrays, 1976, £2.25. Complete book of church flower decoration and organization, including large-scale mechanics.

Flowers in Praise, Julia Clements, Batsford, 1977, £5.95. Useful pictures of flowers in churches.

The Complete Book of Flower Preservation, Geneal Condon, Hale, 1974, £3.00. Includes period arrangements.

Flower Arrangement—Free Style, Edith Brack, Whitehorn Press, £2.20. Modern-style designs.

Design with Plant Material, Marian Aaronson, Grower Books, 1972, £3.15. Modern and abstract designs.

The Craft of Flower Arrangement, Jean Taylor, Stanley Paul, 1976, £2.95 and £1.45. A book for the absolute beginner with little equipment.

Flower Arranging, Violet Stevenson, Hamlyn, 1969, 75p. A beginner's book; very colourful.

Practical Flower Arranging,
Jean Taylor, Hamlyn, 1973,
£2.25.
Beginner-to-intermediate-stage
book; comprehensive and
colourful.

**Japanese Flower
Arrangement,** Norman
Sparnon, Tuttle (Tokyo), £7.50.

**The Art of Japanese Flower
Arranging,** Stella Coe, Barrie
and Jenkins, 1964, £3.00.
By Britain's leading expert.

Pressed Flower Pictures,
Pamela McDowell, Lutterworth,
1969, £3.25.

**BOOKS ON PLANT
MATERIAL**
**Reader's Digest
Encyclopaedia of Garden
Plants and Flowers,** Reader's
Digest, 1971, £7.50.
Excellent identification and
cultural hints arranged
alphabetically and in colour.

**Flower Arranging from Your
Garden,** Sheila Macqueen
Ward Lock, 1977, £4.95.
How to choose plants for
growing for flower arrangement;
with cultural hints.

Planting for Pleasure, Jean
Taylor, Stanley Paul, 1973,
£2.00 and £1.00.
Basic cultural instructions and
flower arrangement.

Growing Flowers, Janet
Browne, Macdonald
Educational, 1977, £1.

Indoor Plants, Brian Ward and
Tom Wellstead, Macdonald
Educational, 1978, £1.

**A Gardener's Dictionary of
Plant Names,** A. W. Smith,
Cassell, 1972, £3.25.
An invaluable checklist.

Garden Terms Simplified,
A. J. Huxley, David and Charles,
1971, £1.25.

Pictorial Gardening, Hamlyn,
£2.25.
Good illustrations of gardening
skills.

**Botany for Flower
Arrangers,** John Tampion and
Joan Reynolds, Pelham Books,
1971, £2.10.
Explains reasons for various
techniques in conditioning.

Nature as Designer, Bertel
Bager, Warne, 1971, £4.00.
A botanical art study.

Foliage Plants, Christopher
Lloyd, Collins, 1973, £2.80.

**Garden Foliage for Flower
Arrangement,** Sybil Emberton,
Faber, 1968, £2.60.

**Flower Arranging in House
and Garden,** George Smith,
Pelham Books, £5.95.
Flower arrangements in settings
and growing plants.

**Wild Flowers for the
Garden,** Stephen Dealler,
Batsford, 1977, £4.95 and
£3.25.

Wild Flowers of Britain,
Roger Phillips, Ward Lock and
Pan, 1977, £6.50 and £3.95.
Excellent colour photographs
for use in identifying wild
flowers.

The Shell Nature Book,
Grigson and Fisher, Dent, 1964,
£2.75.
Good help in making landscape
arrangements.

MAGAZINES
The Flower Arranger:
quarterly; 30p per issue through
flower arranging clubs; £2.00

per annum mailed to an address
in the United Kingdom including
postage and packing. Overseas
rates: sea mail US $5.00, air
mail US $8.00, or equivalent
currency, mailed anywhere.
From Taylor Bloxham Ltd,
Tyrrell Street, Leicester
LE3 5SB. (Cheques should
be made payable to:
National Association of Flower
Arrangement Societies of Great
Britain—*The Flower Arranger*.)

Flora: quarterly; 50p; from
booksellers and newsagents.
Postal subscription: UK £2.60;
abroad £3 a year, sea mail.

EDUCATIONAL LEAFLETS
These can be obtained from
The National Association of
Flower Arrangement Societies
of Great Britain, 21a Denbigh
Street, London SW1:
telephone 01 828 5145.
The cost is 10p each, plus 10p
packing and postage for single
copies, and 30p for bulk orders.
(Cheques and postal orders
should be made payable to
NAFAS Publications.)
1 'Tools and Equipment for
Flower Arrangement'.
2 'The Care of Cut Flowers
and Foliage'.
3 'Preserving Plant Material
with Glycerine'.
4 'Drying Plant Material'.
5 'The Use of Driftwood'.
6 'Pot-et-fleur'.
7 'Show Work for Beginners'.
8 'Preserving Flowers with
Desiccants'.
9 'Pressed Flower Pictures'.
10 'Foliage for Flower
Arrangers'.
11 'Swags and Plaques'.
12 'Home-made Containers'.
A list of other publications,
including calendars, diaries and
booklets on the more
specialized aspects of flower
arranging in this country, is
available from the same
address.

Glossary

Abstract arrangement: a design in which plant material is not used naturalistically. A decorative abstract makes patterns and is based on the design qualities of plant material. An expressive abstract reflects the arranger's feelings about an abstract subject.

Accessory: anything other than plant material used as part of an arrangement except the base or the container.

Adjacent colours: colours lying next to each other on the colour circle; these are also called analogous colours.

Base: any object on which an arrangement stands.

Candlecup: A cup to attach to a narrow-necked container or candlestick to hold the mechanics.

Colour circle: a diagram to show the relationships between colours.

Colour value: the darkness or lightness of a colour.

Complementary colours: those that lie opposite on the colour circle.

Conditioning: the preparation of cut plant material to take up water, and the filling of plant tissue with water.

Container: the part of an arrangement which holds the plant material, usually the stem ends.

Desiccant: a drying agent.

Design: either a flower arrangement, or the way it is assembled.

Driftwood: wood weathered by the elements—but not necessarily by being immersed in water.

Emphasis point: a dominant part of an arrangement.

Free-form: a type of arrangement free of recognizable geometric outline; also called 'free-style', and sometimes 'modern'.

Hogarth curve: an 'S' shape, named after the English painter William Hogarth.

Hue: a fully saturated, unmodified colour.

Ikebana: the art of Japanese flower arrangement.

Intensity: the degree of concentration of a colour.

Interpretative arrangement: a design in plant material that explains a meaning or tells a story.

Landscape arrangement: a design that interprets a natural scene.

Line arrangement: a design with a dominant linear quality and little plant material.

Line-mass arrangement: a design with a dominant linear quality and an area of massed plant material.

Luminosity: quantity of light emitted via a coloured surface.

Mass arrangement: a design using little inner space.

Mechanics: supports to hold plant material in position in an arrangement.

Medium: the materials of an art or craft.

Modern arrangement: a design of a type originated during the present generation.

Monochromatic: anything of one colour.

Oasis: a trade name for plastic foam used by flower arrangers, but generally applied to any brand.

Pedestal arrangement: a design on a plinth or column usually standing on the floor.

Period arrangement: a design in a style of a past era.

Pinholder: a device having sharp pins embedded in lead on which to impale stems. Also called a *kenzan*, a frog or, a needlepoint holder.

Plant material: any part of a plant, fresh, dried or preserved.

Plaque: a three-dimensional design on a visible background, without a container, made to hang or stand, which can be framed or unframed, with or without glass.

Plastic foam: a material made in blocks for holding stem ends of plant material, with or without the property of retaining water.

Pot-et-fleur: a design of growing plants and cut flowers assembled together.

Preserving: replacing water in plant material with glycerine to retain the shape indefinitely.

Saturation: intensity of colour. A fully saturated colour is free of black, white or grey.

Shade: a hue mixed with black.

Show schedule: a list of the specific requirements for exhibits in a show.

Spectrum: the range of colours produced by diffraction of light.

Swag: a three-dimensional design without a container, assembled on an invisible background or mechanics, to hang up or stand.

Tint: a hue mixed with white.

Tone: a hue mixed with black and white. A dark tone contains more black, and a light tone, more white. This term is also used to refer generally to any variation of colour.

Traditional arrangement: a classical style originating in a previous generation.

Triad: a colour scheme using three colours equidistant on the colour circle, and/or their tints, tones and shades.

Well pinholder: a pinholder built into a container to hold water.

Western arrangement: a style that originated in the Western world.

Index

Numbers in italics indicate illustrations

Credits

Artists

Pamela Dowson
Ron Hayward Art Group
Oxford Illustrators
Anne Isseyegh
Vanessa Luff
John Shackell
Ralph Stobart

Photographs

Bernard Alfieri: 7 (bottom)

Amateur Gardening: 11
Edith Brack: 55 (left)
Pat Brindley: 10, 54 (bottom
   left, top left and right)
British Museum: contents, 14,
   15 (top)
Cheshire Life: 18
Julia Clements: 8 (bottom), 55
   (right), 63, 76
Sonia Halliday: contents, 15
   (bottom)
Daisy Hayes: 6, 19
Leslie Johns: 37
NAFAS/*The Flower Arranger*:
   20, 58, 59, 62, 72 (right), 73,
   79

National Gallery, London: 16
National Trust: contents, 72
   (left)
Graham Powell Studios: 4
Radio Times Hulton Picture
   Library: 17
Syndication International: 60,
   61
Jean Taylor: 5, 7 (top), 8 (top),
   9, 24, 54 (bottom right), 64,
   65
Thames Television: 45, 47, 77

Cover

Photograph: Paul Forrester
Design: Barry Kemp